Globalization of Concern

Volume I

AIDAN G. MSAFIRI

Dar es Salaam University Press

Published by
Dar es Salaam University Press
P.O. Box 35182
Dar es Salaam
TANZANIA

© Aidan G. Msafiri, 2008

ISBN: 978-9976-60-481-8

All rights reserved. No part of this publication may be reproduced or transmitted in any form or any means, electronic or mechanical, including photocopying, or any information storage and retrieval system without written permission from Dar es Salaam University Press.

Contents

Acknowledgements..*v*
Foreword ....*vi*
Preamble..*ix*

CHAPTER ONE
Economic Globalisation and Justice in Africa 1

Preamble..2
   The Real Picture of Economic Injustices..........................6
   Some Ideological and Philosophical Roots 12
   Toward A Transformative and Better Paradigm.............16
   Some Concluding Remarks: Which Way Forward?......22

CHAPTER TWO
Rethinking About the Role of the Church on the HIV/AIDS and the Post ARVCrises: A Tanzanian Perspective 26
   Status Quaestionis..27
   The HIV/AIDSAnd Post Arv Treatment Challenges Today..31
   Rethinking Beyond Demographic and Statistical............35
   Concluding Theses and Benchmarks: Which Way Forward?..42

CHAPTER THREE
Natural Law Ethics and Consumerism Today 50
   Prolegomena 51
   Justification..52

Scope, Vision and Structure of the Work..................................53
Some Anthropologico-Philosophical and Ideological
Roots, Signposts and World Views for Consumerism
Today..54
Utilitarianism and Consumerist Culture 57
The Neo-Liberatist Argument and Consumerism.....................58
The Unlimited Economic and Technological Growth
Argument and Consumerism...58
Environmental (Ecological) Destruction and Consumerism...........59
Commodification of Religious and Liturgical Feasts and
Celebrations..61
The Post-Modern Communication's Technology and
Consumerism..62
Natural Law Ethics (Ratio Ethica) and Consumerism 63
Rethinking About The Role of Ratio Ethical Against
Consumerism..68

Chapter Four
Women and the Unfair Distribution of Resources and Wealth in Tanzania 73
Aim..73
Statement of the Problem: What is the Issue at Stake?...............74
Justification...75
Some Socio-economic, Gender Injustices in Tanzania....................76
Womens' Worst Enemies: A Broader Picture 80
Which Way Forward?..82

Chapter Five
The Anatomy of Witchcraft and Its Impact on Human Life in Tanzania Today 88
Preliminary Remarks...88
The Anatomy of Witchcraft: Deeper Causes 90
Some Concluding Remarks, Reflections and
Recommendations..99

Acknowledgements

This volume is an outcome of God's love in my academic carrier and reflection at St. Augustine's University of Tanzania in particular.

First, I wish to express my sincere thanks to Almighty God for His abundant graces and love to me.

Second, I wish to express my heartfelt gratitudes to my parents and all my life-long academic mentors todate. I also wish to thank my Austria friends and benefactors who enabled the publication of this book.

Third, I am highly grateful to St. Augustine University of Tanzania authorities; professors, lecturers, students and workers for their invaluable solidarity and cooperation.

My special thanks also go to Prof. Robert White for re-reading the manuscript and for giving his professional insights.

I also wish to express my deepest thanks to Dr. Michael Kadeghe of the University of Dar es Salaam for writing a foreword to this book. Last, but not least, sincere gratitudes go to Professor Harald Mandl of Vienna, Austria for his great inspiration to me. May God ever bless and reward you all.

Foreword

This book is a momentous contribution to the ongoing contentious discussions on the concept and effects of globalization, particularly on the socioeconomic life of the less developed countries like Tanzania. In handling globalization concerns, the author uses interdisciplinary and multidisciplinary approaches including socio-ethical paradigms as well as contemporary economic theories. The term "globalization" has of recent become one of the most fashionable buzzwords of contemporary, economic political and academic debate. In popular discourse, globalization often functions as little more than a synonym for one or more of the following phenomena: the pursuit of classical liberal (or "free market") policies in the world economy ("economic liberalization"), the growing dominance of western (or even American) forms of political, economic, and cultural life ("westernization" or "Americanization"), the proliferation of new information technologies (the "Internet Revolution"), as well as the notion that humanity stands at the threshold of realizing one single unified community in which major sources of social conflict have vanished(global integration).

Fortunately, the author of this book goes further than the above definitions by formulating a precise and empirical concept of globalization by posing a critical examination on the relationship between globalization and poverty. Given the current reshaping of social life activities globally, the author looks at the impact on issues related to gender, social justice, morality, equity, human rights, religious ethics, and virulent diseases. He views globalization as the rising tide that lifts all boats at the same time and yet destroys all non-prepared boats.

The book demonstrates how the neo-liberal economic paradigm stresses justification for ruthless exploitation of the poor, neglecting ethical values and truth of needs and wants of universal human beings. The author reiterates that globalization has resulted to failure, thus generating more poverty, more crises worldwide, more money flowing from poor to rich countries, leaving poor countries with more debts that they can hardly manage.

The author stresses that globalization did not evolve in any natural economic way; it has been an artificial economic forced march, led by elite groupings in governments, large corporations and international entities surrounding the world banks. The main tool of globalization is called "Free Trade", which is not really trade. The main commodities of "Free Trade" are workers who are put on a world trading block to compete with each other for the same jobs and same resources. Since globalization contains far-reaching implications for virtually every facet of human life, the author suggests the need to rethink key questions of normative political theory which will shade light on alternatives leading to equal level of global socioeconomic competition.

Going through the five well argued chapters of this book, the reader will realize that globalization is yet another form of veiled imperialism aimed at, not only impoverishing the destitute, but also destroying the ethos of human beings. Chapter three which is on "Natural Law Ethics" uncovers such behaviors as greediness, excessive accumulation of materials and egoism; elements which, according to the author, have inevitably led to class antagonisms and social annihilation. Human beings are said to be inclined towards "having" rather than "being" a neurotic insatiable tendency which, from the Natural Law Ethics, leads to exploitative relations. The global ethics education initiative should advocate for building better international social and economic structures so as to promote social justice which, for two decades now, has been dwarfed by, *inter alia*, evils of globalization.

I would wish to recommend this book to a wider audience it deserves given its unique relevance. The book will indubitably be highly commendable as a textbook for ethics to higher institutions of learning, colleges and university students, as well as the general public. In short, the author quests for an alternative and a better model of globalization.

Dr. Michael Kadeghe
Senior Lecturer
University of Dar es Salaam

October, 2008

Preamble

Undoubtedly, the word "globalization" has become one the most disputable idol – jargons of the 21st Century. Quite often, it is loaded with too pessimistic overtones and implications. Truly, globalization entails a multiplicity of both positive and negative trends and connotations. However, this Anglo-Saxon term "globalization" and its French equivalent "mondialisation" needs to be juxtaposed with the Greek word "Oikos" which essentially means a common household.

To its proponents, the process of globalization is considered to be a grace and an absolutely necessary universal "credo" to be hailed and embraced so as to become richer and richer. Hence, emphasizing "having more" than "being more." It makes a minority of the world population approximately 20% "great winners." On the other hand, the protagonists of globalization, constituting about 70% of the world population simply consider it as disgrace and therefore an excuse to global justice and welfare as a whole. They simply view it as the causative element for the ever widening gap between the rich and the poor world wide. For them, it works in favour of the fastest. That is, "the survival of the fastest."

Objectively seen, globalization encapsulates great chances as well as risks to peoples and the earth. Consequently, there is urgent need to search for a better paradigm of globalization. We need a ***globalization of concern*** especially in sensitizing humanity on the potential risks, threats and challenges entailed in the driving forces of the 21st Century process of globalization. We need a globalization of justice, health, peace, welfare, human dignity, rights, values just to mention a few. Globalization of concern as echoed in this volume is an alternative and better paradigm which essentially cares and promotes holistic justice and more so addresses the fundamental threats on people's cultures lives and the mother earth as a whole. In short, both humans and non-humans not only today and tomorrow but for the far fetched future as a whole. This new paradigm could briefly be called AGAPE model of globalization. That is "**Alternative Globalisation Addressing Peoples and the Earth.**"

This volume (volume one) is a collection of academic presentations and discussions expressing the spirit and courage of "concern" on some different current socio-ethical threats and challenges especially from a Tanzanian (African) context. The methodology used is profoundly interdisciplinary and multidisciplinary. These papers were presented at different national and international academic fora and symposia from 2005 to 2008. A second volume is hoped to come after this. As regards it objectives as well as justification, this book tries to call for a collective concern and solidarity in responding to the ever worsening threats and challenges to human life, health, justice, dignity, rights, cultures, environment and the poorest of the poor in Tanzania in particular and Africa in general. Conversely, it calls for a credible globalization of human solidarity and concern before reaching the *"Point of no Return."* Now we are at the *"Last Point of Return!"*

Briefly stated, we therefore need to globalize fundamental human and social values, justice, solidarity, concern, care, fairness, truthfulness, accountability and transparency locally and world wide. Thus, *local thinking and global acting*. Admittedly, competition as a key driving force of globalization needs to go hand in hand with true cooperation. As Rob van Drimmelen (1998) aptly comments, one "of the hallmarks of globalization is increased and almost ruthless competition", we need to critique its reductionist and manipulative tricks. Hence, creating a new formula and "Modus Operandi" for a credible and meaningful way forward. We need ethics of globalization too.

Indeed, this first volume can definitely be used as a manual especially in teaching social ethics in different universities and institutes of higher learning particularly in Tanzania and East Africa, Africa and world wide. With such views and passionate concern among others, African scholars, politicians, economists, ethicists, sociologists, mass communicators and all professionals from all walks of life cannot estrange themselves especially from the essential needs of fellow humans and the earth. These need to fully address and respond to the current local and global crises and challenges hard hitting humanity as a whole. As the adage goes, "the business of business is business," more than ever before, scholars, today there is urgent need to develop and acquire a true culture of courage and concern for others and with others especially the poor and the marginalized. These include welfare fellow humans and that of the environment. This work aims precisely to initiate this process and culture of globalizing constructive and transformative attitudes and culture.

As regards its structure, this work contains five chapters. In chapter one, an attempt is made to expose the challenges entailed in economic globalization and justice in Tanzania in particular.

The second chapter explores the role and need of the church rethink anew in responding to the HIV/AIDS and the Post ARV crises today.

Chapter three tries to unveil the ever growing consumerist culture in the contemporary society today. In chapter four, effort is made to make a critical analysis and a way forward particularly in finding deep solutions agianst the unfair distribution of resources among women. The last chapter (chapter five), tries to explore the anatomy of witchcraft and its impact on human life particularly contemporary Tanzania.

All these themes occasion impending inter alia socio-economic, ethical, cultural, human and medical crises. These need urgent and proper solutions or alternatives.

Let us all not simply talk the talk, but walk the walk. Truly, we still have a long way to go. One step today initiates the entire process and journey.

Chapter One

ECONOMIC GLOBALISATION AND JUSTICE IN AFRICA: QUEST FOR A BETTER PARADIGM?

Abstract

The search for a radically different, better and a transformative economic paradigm world wide is a *conditio sine qua non* for a just Africa. Undoubtedly, something is ethically questionable when at the eve of this Century, 20% of population is consuming 83% of world's riches while the rest that is 17% of global wealth is only accessible to 80% of global population, Africa included. (Refer the Champagne Glass Economy). Definitely, from a socio-ethical and economic perspectives the logic, nature and goal of the current paradigm of economic globalization is diametrically opposed particularly to the universal human ethical values, principles, norms maxims and criteria. Among others, these include the principles of justice, equality, solidarity, abundant life (John 10:10), "*utu*" (dignity) as well as true Agape (Mt 22:37-40).

The neo-liberal economic paradigm aims at maximization of profit regardless of ethical values and truths. It has a systemic negative impact particularly for the poor and Africa in particular. This paper specifically tries to give a socio-ethical critique of the present paradigm of economic globalization with its destructive impact particularly on Africa.

It therefore tries to suggest "a better" or "a different" kind of globalization which will promote not mere economic growth but more so universal human values of equality, freedom, partnerships, fraternity, holistic peace, ecological justice dignity to mention a few. In this sense, adopting the adage, "the business of business is business." Nonetheless, we ought to embark on "a different but a better business." We need to globalize good ethical values against the destructive ones. As African Christians, scholars and ethical "periti" we are called to play this multi-facetted transformation particularly in the light of the basic socio-ethical and religious belief and commitments we cherish. In brief, Africa needs to embark on a different and better form of globalization for a more just, compassionate and sustainable world as a whole.

Preamble

Status Quaestionis

The systemic unjust impact and effects of the neoliberal paradigm of economic globalization for Africa in particular cannot be exaggerated. It's inner motive and basic operation are profoundly based on the maximization of profit regardless of any socio-ethical human or existential considerations. As a key and integral component of the entire process of liberalization economic globalization involves a cut-throat competition with "great losers" and "great winners."

It discourages the formers and empowers the later. The *modus operandi* of this paradigm encapsulates philosophical as well as ideological worldviews and rules of the jungle. That is, the survival of the fittest and fastest particularly in the spheres of trade, market, finance, information and knowledge. Undoubtedly this philosophical stance constitutes the essence of this paradigm.

Justification

From an African viewpoint in particular, economic globalization exacerbates wanton disparities and remarkable injustices between and within the poor and the rich. It homogenizes and hegemonizes human life, ethics and businesses. Consequently it cannot simply be taken wholesale. It needs to be criticized. As the dictum goes the business of business is business, the neoliberal paradigm of economic globalization needs to be transformed and replaced with better alternatives. Christoph Stueckelberger (2002) observes that economic globalization "must be our goal if it involves an attempt to understand the world as one mankind one ecosystem together with their interdependence as long as it envisions fertile ground supporting life in dignity with a fair share for everyone"[1] He goes on reaffirming the philosophical and existential altruism that it "must be rejected if it involves an attempt to reduce the world's multiplicity to one standardized economic, cultural and political model which is created by only a few agents and in which the economy has priority over any other sphere of life and action."[2] Unfortunately, today, there has been too much discussions and talk at different global economic (e.g. the WTO, World Bank, IMF Conferences in Doha, Quatar, Washington Davos, etc.) for insisting on the monolithic current model as the only panacea for growth and poverty eradication.

Definitely this model has both strengths and weaknesses. Its weaknesses need to be challenged. Its logic and philosophy needs to be radically changed and transformed. Hence, quest for new and "better alternatives – of transformative justice, global solidarity and "agape". Conversely the lives of the "anawim" (the poor and marginilised and the ecosphere) world wide and Africa in particular must not be endangered by the ideology of free trade power domination, profit and mere economic growth propelled by the promises of the current paradigm of economic globalization. More than ever before, today, African ethicists, scholars, politicians, economists need to challenge the destructive philosophical and economic worldviews and trends of "the survival of the fittest and fastest" as well as "I am because consume" with better alternatives. Among others at this juncture, Rene de Cartes' dictum: "I think therefore I am" needs to be reconsidered.

---

[1] Christoph Stueckelbelger, Global Trade Ethics (Geneva: WCC Publication, 2002) 19.
[2] Ibid p.19.

Today for instance something must philosophically, ethically as well as epistemologically radically be wrong when "1.5 billion citizen of our planet – the majority of whom are women, children and Indigenous people live on less than one dollar a day, even as the world's richest 20 percent account for 86 percent of global consumption of goods and services. The annual income of the richest 1% is equal to that of the poorest 57%, and 24,000 die each day from poverty and malnutrition. Environmental problems of global warming depletion of natural resources and loss of biodiversity loom ever larger...."[3] From an African viewpoint, Samwel Kobia (2003) considers the crux of the neoliberal paradigm of economic globalization as being in its "inherent socio-economic injustices that have resulted in and continue to impoverish the poor. Globalization like slavery is an oppressive system that denies people their right of economic and social independence, indeed, their right to life.... Its commodification and its unethical measurement of life only in dehumanized economic parameters cannot go unchallenged."[4]

Scope and Vision

This chapter searches for a radically "different" or "better" form of economic globalization. It tries to particularly address not only the traditional economic roots and motives of the current paradigm but more so the deep seated philosophical worldviews and ideological benchmarks. Unfortunately so far the trend and focus has mostly been on consequential neoliberal economic causes and parameters rather than the causative philosophical and ideological worldviews and convictions. In other words we cannot achieve "a better" or different model of economic globalization without an indepth overview of its inner driving

---

[3] World Council of Churches, JPC Team, *Alternative Globalization: Addressing People and Earth* (Geneva: WCC Publications 2005) 8-9.
[4] Kobia Samuel, *The Courage to Hope* (Geneva: WCC Publications 2003) 142.

philosophical roots and worldviews. As a profoundly interdisciplinary perennial quest for true paradigmatic shift of the current neoliberal paradigm of economic globalization. I envisage therefore, a radically new and transformative paradigm based on new economic, philosophical and ethical truths and values. However, it is a perennial ethical critique investigation and reflection. It entails a synopsis of three key but brief parts. That is, empirical, philosophical and ethical.

The Structure

It entails three major parts. The first offers a brief but concrete picture and critique particularly of some economic injustices poignant characteristics of the current economic paradigm both nationally (in Tanzania) and globally. The second part tries to explore the deep seated philosophical root worldviews and benchmarks this kind of economic globalization. The third part tries to integrate entire edifice by underpinning the key ethical as well as theological components visions for a better and different economic globalization. Hence, I envisage and suggest "a better" or "a different" kind or "alternative" to economic globalization today. In this sense, the dictum "the business of business is business" will come true. Nonetheless this is neither one person's business nor scholars' business. It is everybody's business.

As African Christians, scholars and ethical "periti" in particular, we have the mission and obligation to ignite this quest and process towards a better paradigm as globalization is unavoidable. Among others, " a better business" will necessarily engage us to both globalize and localize universal human values of true justice, preservation of life, solidarity, dignity holistic peace, tolerance, trust, partnership, preservation of life responsibility, freedom, transparency, integrity, accountability fair trade, fair taxation, fair profit, fair pay, fair speed, forgiveness to and more so true "agape". Indeed, these should be therefore be the foundational elements of our esteemed alternative vision for another world built on a new set of values encapsulated and holistic justice, human dignity and agape.

EMPIRICAL PART

The Real Picture of Economic Injustices: Some Examples

A (Local) Tanzanian Perspective

The Agricultural Sector

Tanzanian's economy depends for foreign earnings, largely on export of cash crops particularly coffee, tea, sugar, pyrethrum, sisal, cashewnuts and tobacco. The 2004 Economic survey shows a notable increase in cash crop production "from 603.840.6 tons in 2003 to 829.994.0 tons in 2004 equivalent to an increase of 37.5 percent."[5] The table below generally testifies this sectorial and economic truth.

Agricultural Exports

Crop	2003	2004	% Increase – Tons ('000) Change 2003/04
Cotton	190,153	344,207	81.0
Tobacco	32,693.62	51,972	58.9
Sugar	190,120	223,889	17.8
Tea	28,028	30,259	7.9
Pyrethrum	3,000	897	(70.1)
Coffee	46,205	51,970	12.5
Sisal	23,641	26,800	13.4
Cashewnuts	90,000	100,000	11.1
TOTAL	603,841	829,994	37.5

Source: *Crop Boards (2004)*

Interpretation

First, despite this sectorial growth, generally, the prices of most of these cash crops have simultaneously a significant fall at the world

---

[5] The United Republic of Tanzania, The President's Office -The Economic Survey 2004 (Dar es Salaam – June 2005), 130.

markets. For instance, one kilogram of raw Arabica Coffee from Kilimanjaro Tanzania is locally sold at Tsh. 500/= or half a dollar (1 US Dollar = 1,050/= Tsh. – Exchange Rate February 2006). However, the same coffee is being sold at 9 US Dollars to the global coffee dealers and buyers in the United States. This is equivalent to Tsh. 9,450/= as net profit!

Second as Africa and Tanzania in particular are being continuously integrated into this free "global business on economy" propelled by the philosophy of free market laws and unfair competition her agricultural exports constantly face huge and unending obstacles. This is particularly due to the heavily subsidized agricultural as well as livestock products in the rich North – North-American and North Atlantic countries.[6] This scenario is poignant to unequal rules, unfair prices, unfair speed, and unfair competition leading eventually to unfair remuneration of neoliberal economic globalization. This applies not only to Tanzania's (Africa's) agricultural exports but also to industrial fishing as well as mining exports. Hence survival of fittest and fastest! Again these are representative and symptomatic of the entire crisis. Further more, even diversification does not guarantee the best results. Hence the need to search for a new vision and alternatives to economic globalization particularly for Africa.

Third, Wagwe and Musonda (2002), claim that "Many developing poor countries including Tanzania, have not created a conducive environment for firms to compete in the global market. The weakness of many developing countries in this area has resulted in a lack of competitiveness of their firms, leading to divestitures, privatization and even closer of firms that cannot compete. Closures mean a loss of employment opportunities...."[7]

---

[6] Benjamin W. Mkapa, *Address to Officially Open the AMECEA Fourteenth Plenary: Challenge to Preserve Humanity in AFER* – Special Issue Gaba Publications Eldoret October – December 2002 – Vol. 44- Numbers 5 & 6 page 222.

[7] S.M. Wangwe, Musonda F.M. "*Local Perspectives on Globalization. The Economic Domain*": *Research on Poverty Alleviation* (Dar es Salaam, Mkuki na Nyota Publishers, 2002), 69.

The Fishing Industry and Ecological Injustices: Example of Lake Victoria
Besides agricultural exports, and the resultant massive economic injustices to Tanzania farmers, fishing activities around Lake Victoria is a case in point. Economically, Lake Victoria and its basin have great socio-economic and environmental potential not only to the three East African countries of Tanzania, Kenya and Uganda but also to Nile basin countries. It is endowed with abundant natural resources marine fish like the Nile Perch "Tilapia" other fish and marine riches, biodiversity, fresh water, wild life, minerals, hydroelectric power, agricultural and tourist potentials to mention some.[8]

However, Lake Victoria is subject to a serious environmental hazards including drastic decrease in fish spread of destructive algae and water hyacinth, illegal fishing methods, and massive industrial pollution and waster.[9] From an ethical point of view, this carries a monstrous injustice which needs to be addressed and challenged.

First from the economic point of view recent research observations in Mwanza city 2006 testify that due to massive exports of fish fillet products from Lake Victoria in particular the local prices have simply sky rocketed making them unaffordable to many local people around the Lake Zone. For example, one kilogram of Nile Perch fish is sold at Tsh. 1,200/= or one US dollar. The prices of Tilapia fish are even higher. This has forced most of the poor people to resort in buying fish scraps locally known as "panki" A piece of "panki" is being sold between Tshs. 200/= and 300/=. This is diametrically opposed to the demands of needs-related justice. It pauperizes the local populace and enriches the well-to-do abroad.

Second, from an ecological point of view, such unsustainable depletion of Lake Victoria's fish resources and biodiversity is contrary

---

[8] Arcado D. Ntagazwa, *Welcome Statement to the Lake Victoria Environment Project – Scientific Conference* 6 – 10 August, 2001 in Mwanza. Vice President's Office page vii.

[9] Aidan G. Msafiri, *The African Ecological Crisis As A Theological and Ethical Challenge A Case Study in Tanzania* (Unpublished Ph.D. Dissertation Vienna, 2003)2-14.

to the demands of ecological justice. In its broadest and deepest sense; Christoph Stueckelberger (2002) considers justice pertaining to ecology as "a sustainable use and fair distribution of resources as well as a reduction in and a fair distribution of ecological burdens. One of the prerequisites for ecological justice is the cost of transparency in relation to goods"[10]

A Global Perspective

From a global view, there is a cause and link effect between economic and ecological injustices and economic globalization. The three are profoundly interrelated and interdependent. Among others, the following examples are poignant to this global unjust scenario.

The Economic Injustices of the Global Champagne Economy

First, the champagne glass economy below is indicative of the ever growing scarred economic inequalities and unfair distribution of global riches today. It indicates that the top 20% North-Atlantic and American countries consumes 83% of all world's wealth, while the next 20% of world populace have accessibility to only to 11% of global riches and lastly the remaining 60% have simply an access to 6% of the world's wealth.[11] The same wanton inequalities apply also in the areas of resources linked with soil flora and fauna, trade, finance, knowledge, power, information capital, corporate and business labour. Hence, giving rise to huge unemployment, generic workers de-nationalization of and de-materialization of global products, as well as "cassinonization" of economy.

---

[10] Christoph Stueckelberger, *Global Trade Ethics* p. 48.

[11] Justice Peace and Creation Team, WCC – *Alternative Globalization Addressing People and Earth* (AGAPE) (Geneva: WCC Publications, 2005), 10.

The Champagne Glass Economy

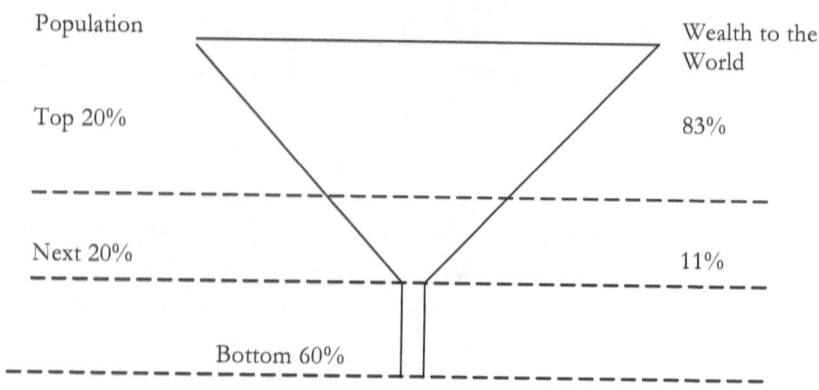

Source: *Justice Peace and Creation Team WCC, 2005*

Second, from a global point of view, the neoliberal champagne glass economy systemically hegemonises and homogenizes life and economy. Using its logic of unlimited consumption and economic growth, it plunders the earth under the auspices of short term sustainability and gain. The belief that corporate free market, economic growth can sustain development is per se illusive and unrealistic. It is diametrically opposed to the basic tenets and demands of ecological justice and the ethical principle of sustainability. It accelerates the depletion of non renewable natural resources nationally and globally. As a super profit oriented neoliberal ideology, economic globalization systematically commodifies and privatizes everything on the globe and worst of all public goods such as water, soil flora and fauna land. Sooner or later even air will be privatized world wide. For Africa and poor indigenous peoples in a particular, the ecological impact is simply disastrous.

Third, but not least, the current problem of climate change is per excellence a justice issue. It has recently been claimed that massive air traffic and intercontinental transport of goods has remarkably contributes to global warming and deterioration of the environment. In this regard, Maria (2001) is worth paraphrasing. He claims that these transport operations have no rational explanation for high environmental costs they give rise to. For example, there is the case of 1 Kg. of grapes from California being transported by plane to Germany in a journey that causes an emission of 20kg of CO_2 in the atmosphere or it happens too that, crabs fished in the North Sea are taken to Morocco to be shelled and then to Poland to be packed before reaching the markets of Hamburg."[12] The same destructive phenomon as far as eco-justice is concerned takes place around the Lake Zone in the East and Central African Zone. Almost daily air cargo planes fly in and out to Mwanza, Kampala, Jinja and Kisumu cities for fish and fish products to European, Asian and North American fish markets. Quite often such air cargo planes are outmoded and substandard. Hence, causing maximum amount of air pollution.

Last but not least, as far as another dimension of eco-justice is concerned, the unsustainable high consumption of fossil fuel e.g. "mkaa" (charcoal) and oil especially in many cities of the developing world for instance Dar es Salaam, Kampala, Nairobi, Lusaka, Maputo, Bujumbura and Kigali increases environmental catastrophes to communities and peoples lives especially those living around coastal areas and islands. These are highly exposed to severe floods, storms and drought spells. The untold consequences of climate changes and global warming are indicative of ecological injustices due to global warming. Findings show that in 20 years time, the entire ice cap or glacier on top of the Kilimanjaro the highest mountain in Africa will vanish. Let us now try to identify the basic philosophical and ideological roots behind the neoliberal economic paradigm.

---

[12] Josep F. Maria, In CJ Booklets Globalization: "Ah, Yes...It is a Marvelous Excuse for Many Things (*Barcelona: CJ Booklets*, 2001, Vol. 100), 12.

ANTHROPOLOGICAL PART

Some Ideological and Philosophical Roots of Economic Globalisation

Definitely, the quest for better and more viable and transformative alternatives to the current neoliberal model of economic globalization needs to go deeper and beyond mere economic parameters and criteria. Among others, this necessarily involves particularly the search for the deep ideological and philosophical worldviews, "arguments" and benchmarks of economic globalization. The following in particular deserve special attention.

The Modern Consumerist Ideology and Philosophy

The world today is (largely) being driven by ever growing and unsatiable stimuli for excessive consumerism and materialism. Philosophically, there is a radical paradigmatic geo-economic shift from "I think therefore I am" to "I consume (buy) therefore I am." Cortina and Carreras (2004) make this observation: "it is no longer a question of goods that are basic and necessary but rather the current trend is in buying superfluous unnecessary gods."[13] This includes an array of all sorts of new types and fashions of consumer goods produce foodstuffs, whereby its "justification" affirms "mteja ni mfalme" (the customer is the king). The mushrooming of huge supermarkets as well as big gigantic shopping Malls especially in North America, Western Europe and Asia (China) today is a clear and vivid testimony. In today's turbo consumerist world, many simply buy what they want and not what they need! Hence, giving rise a "throw away" consumer society exalting both the power of the consumer and the dictatorship of manufacturers.

---

[13] Adela Cortina, Ignasi Carreras, "I Buy Therefore I Am," (Barcelona: CJ Booklets, 2004, Vol. 116) 4.

The Extreme Anthropocentrism and Individualism

This is new form of ideological worldview. It perceives humans as rulers, lords, master "exploiters," "loci" (centre) as well as "telos" (destiny) of all economic activity. The world and economy are simply considered to be for the service of humans and not vice versa. The human person is simply considered to be a "homo faber" (producer). Such an extremist and dualist view of the world legitimizes any indiscriminate subjugation of fellow humans and the cosmos. It is characteristic of an anthropology of neoliberal capitalism. It ignores both the dignity and worth of human beings as well as the interdependence and interconnectedness between humans and the rest of the universe. On the practical level therefore, it essentially causes a dichotomy pertaining to the principles of economic justice and ecological sustainability as a whole. Briefly, it upholds the principle of excessive individuality at the expense of the communitarian truths in trade, finance, power and profit.

Neoliberalism as a Religion and Idol

One of the basic tenets of the neoliberalism is the aspect of economic fanaticism and fundamentalism.[14] The key aspects of the neoliberal ideology of economic globalization particularly trade, market, finance, media, property, capital and money are viewed by many as "the reigning" of god today. They occasion a sort of a "messiah" and a "messianic" breakthrough. Their authority and power are simply absolute. As William Greider (1997) succinctly comments, "many intelligent people have come to worship these market principles, like a spiritual code that will revolve all the larger questions for us as long as no one interferes with its authority."[15]

---

[14] Javier Victoria, "*A Just Economic Order, CJ Booklets* Barcelona 1998 p.10. as He quotes Sebastian L. *Rich World, Poor World*, Sal Terrae, Santander, 1992 p. 102.

[15] William Greider, *One World Ready or Not: The Manic Logic of Global Capitalism*, (New York: Simon and Schuster, 1997), 473.

Harvey Cox (1999) deeply challenges the idolatrous character of market economy by making the following assertion. He says "now the market is becoming more like Yahweh of the Old Testament… to convert into commodities… a radical desacralization that dramatically alters human beings and nature for the sake of higher profits."[16]

As such, as a religion, neoliberalism demands humans to blindly accept its rules, formulae and economic "truths" and "creeds" and the propositions of economic experts as if they were revealed truths. In this regard analogically Robert Levine considers the neoliberal free market ideology as a contemporal form of "monotheism."[17]

The Absolute Competitiveness and Excessive Materialism Ideology

Powerful market principles of free competition, risk, efficiency, and acquisive materialism are increasingly becoming a dominant economic ideology of our times. As such anyone questioning their ethical justification is simply considered as a modern heretic.[18] There are three key tenets to this ideology. First, it accentuates economic Darwinism. That is the, survival of the fittest. World wide, the pace of corporate mergers is astronomic in every sphere of economic undertaking (e.g KLM + N. West Airline, NBC & the ABSA Group Ltd. etc.) Hence, the swallowing up of small fish by the big ones. Second, it goes a step further beyond economic Darwinism. That means, not only the "survival of the fittest," but "the survival of the fastest." Third, it underpins the materialistic view of today's being implies having." Therefore it blindly legitimizes the unvirtuous inner inclinations in human person "amor habendi crescit habendo" (lit. the love of having

---

[16] Harvey Cox, "*The Market as God,*" *The Atlantic Monthly,* (March, 1999) 20.
[17] Robert Levine, in *International Harald Tribune,* July 18-19, (1998), 6.
[18] Rogate R. Mshana (ed) in *Search of a Just Economy in an Article,* "Alternatives to Economic Globalisation* (Geneva: WCC Publications, 2003), 100.

grows with having). In this sense "Homo Sapiens" is at the point of no return simply being rendered into mere "homo oeconomicus or homo faber." That is a mere producer! Further more, its modus operandi is maximization of profit through an oligopoly of absolute power. Definitely, its consequential impact and effect are simply insurmountable giving rise to permanently "great loosers" and "great winners."

The Mechanistic and Functionalistic Views of Ecology (Environment)

Western views of ecology uphold massive egocentrism on the human person. They promote exploitation and manipulation non-humans. Commenting from an African point of view, Harvey Sindima, (1990) says the "mechanistic concept of the world and its attendant manner of living inundated with greed has ruined our vision and interaction with nature."[19] John S. Pobee too, observers that Western thoughts about nature are through and through individualistic and mechanistic in nature. On the practical level, such deep seated ecological world views, have far reaching destructive effects on environment, and the entire web of life as a whole.[20] Moreover, the current economic trend for the commodification and instrumentalisation of human love, beauty, sex, water, air and human values, have their genesis mainly from the Western mechanistic and individualistic philosophical world views. Now let us now make an attempt towards transformative alternatives for the current paradigm. Indeed, there are numerous alternatives. Hence, the business of business should necessarily be business.

---

[19] Harvey Sindima, in Charles Birch (ed) et alua: *Liberating Life "Community of Life"* (MaryKnoll, New York: Orbis Books, 1990), 142.

[20] John S. Pobee, *Celebrating the Jubilee of the World Council of Churches*, (Accra: Assempa Publishers, 1998), 96.

THEOLOGICO – ETHICAL PART

Toward a Transformative and Better Paradigm: "The Business of Business is Business"

Admittedly, in the light of above analysed problematic and unethical effects of the current neoliberal paradigm of economic globalization, among others, theologians, ethicists, scholars, the churches and the entire humanity should search for a "different" and "better" paradigm and alternatives. This quest is particularly encapsulated in the vision that "There Are Numerous Alternatives (TANA) ad opposed to "There Is No Alternative." (TINA) Nonetheless, among others, this necessarily demands an in-depth reflection and transformative socio-economic, ethical political, religious, theological, spiritual business. Thus, implying "the business of business is business." Let us now try to identify the foundational theological-ethical dimensions and benchmarks constitutive of this "new business."

Globalization of Biblical Justice and Solidarity

First, from a Judaeo-Christian tradition, justice is essentially perceived as emanating from God. As a virtue justice necessarily endorses the "suum cuique" principle. That is, "to each and everyone his/her due."[21] In biblical parlance, Michael Schlitt, (1992) considers justice as one of the manifestations of the Christian commandment of love.[22] Indeed the biblical concept of justice is profoundly inspirational and transformative for a better world.

Second, the search for justice necessarily means moving towards those who as the "anawim" (poor) and powerless are being marginalized and tormented by oppressive socio-economic and political systems of the day. Consequently, searching for justice means

---

[21] Robert Spaemann, *Moralische Grundbegriffe* (Muenchen: Beckche Reihe; 1991), 58ff.

[22] Michael Schlitt, "Umweltethik." *Philosophisch-ethische Reflexionen-Theologische Grundlagen Kriterien* (Paderborn: 1992), 2002.

"approaching the poor and powerless living socially and economically marginalized lives and unable to improve their participation and involvement in society by themselves. Social justice rightfully implies advocacy for all those who depend on support and assistance. It does not consist only of personal care for the disadvantaged but aims at dismantling the structural causes for the lack of participation and involvement in social and economic process.[23] The Evangelical Church in Germany, The Common Good and Self – Interest: A Memorandum of the Evangelical Church in Germany, 1991, English Version 1992 paragraph 155.

Third, inspired by Jesus' promise for "life in fullness" and his solidarity with everything (Phil 2: 6-11) Christians, the human community and other life forms, are constantly being called and challenged towards global solidarity and interdependence. This means, on one hand orienting themselves to God and God's solidarity and on the other rejecting the law of the jungle and the neoliberal philosophy of the survival of the fittest and and fastest. We need planetary solidarity or die. Last, Christian churches and ecclesial communities need to restructure the current oppressive socio-economic system in a proactive perspective. Hence Paul M. Zulehner (1990) prophetically warns about oppression of the poor (Ex. 3, 7 – 10) reminds collaboration with aliens widow and orphans (Ex 22: 20 – 30, Dtn. 24: 14f) pay just wages to employees and workers (Dtn. 24: 14ff) and responsibility and care to the entire created world (Gen 1-3, Ps 24: 1, Ps 8: 104).[24]

Globalization of Agape

First, humanity and the Church need to radically transcend beyond the mere demands of cosmic justice. That is, acceptance of Agape

---

[23] The Evangelical Church in Germany, *The Common Good and Self – Interest: A Memorandum of the Evangelical Church in Germany*, 1991, English Version 1992 paragraph 155.

[24] Paul M. Zulehner, *Pastoraltheologies, and Pastorale Futurologie* (Duesseldorf: Patmos Verlag; 1990), 251 – 265.

per se or divine love. Indeed, it empowers concrete and living alternative for a better world. The acceptance of Agape necessarily rejects any form of socio-economic and ecological exclusion, discrimination and exploitation. It promotes and safeguards all life (Jn 1:4, 4:14, 6:35, 10:10, Gal . 2:20, Col. 1:10, Jas 1:12, Rev. 22:2). Moreover on the practical level, globalization of Agape, would mean fulfilling the demands of the Golden Rule (Mt. 22: 37-39) or Great commandment in relationship to humans economy and environment.

Second, Agape vision and alternative embraces the key biblical concepts of Sabbath (Gen. 2: 1-3 Ex. 20:8-11, Lev. 25, Col. 2:16, Luke 23:12) a day of the rest, or a year. It underscores human obligation to observe and respect human and lands rights.[25] The Jubilee year calls and demands humans to be fully responsible for the integrity, peace and reconciliation with all beings, animate and inanimate. It "is a responsibility that must mature on the basis of global dimension of the present ecological crisis and the consequent necessity to meet it a worldwide level since all beings are interdependent in the universal order established by the Creator."[26]

Last, an Agapic stance of life means sharing life at God's table that is, the Agape meal. The Scriptures (Acts 2:42ff and 4:32-35) underpin the early Christian as a community truly sustained by a love and life-nourishing relationships with God and with one another. Indeed, communal meals, festivals, get-together etc. nurture a true culture of hospitality, care, love, equality and life.[27] As a key to a radically transformedlifestyle, the agape-meal challenges every human person to remain united in martyria, diakonia and koinonia. That is witness, service and communion.[28]

---

[25] John S. Pobee, *Celebrating the Jubilee of The World Council of Churches* pp 3-7.

[26] Pontifical Council For Justice and Peace, *Compendium of the Social Doctrine of the Church* (Vatican City: Libreria Editrice Vaticana, 2004), para 466.

[27] Aidan G. Msafiri, "*The Church as Family Model in Africa Theology Today* (Scranton: The University of Scranton Press, 2002),91.

[28] Justice, Peace and Creation Team, World Council of Churches, *Alternative Globalization* pp 15-16.

Globalization From Below

First, among others, there is urgent need today to particularly reverse and thoroughly restructure the key trajectories, contours and operative dynamics of the current neolibral ideology of economic globalization. That means, an economic globalization of people-centred alternatives from below upwards. In this case the market should no longer be considered as the end, but simply a means. It entails and encourages a process of localization or as some calls it "glocolisation." It demands regard to the dignity, expectations, traditions as well as cultures of indigenous people and the poor in particular. Hence, fighting against homogenization of life and economy.

Second, from an African view in particular, there is absolute necessity to particularly re-invent and globalize the "Sokoni" (at-the market place) environment and trade values against the neoliberal free market operations.[29] In many African ethnic groups the "Sokoni" is neither an abstract nor an idolatrous phenomenon. It is occasions an extremely important milieu not only for exchange of goods but more so for communication, safety, interaction and sharing of life. Among others, the following terms among some East African ethnic groups deeply and apply reflect the deeper dynamics and meanings "Sokoni" as a crucial place of sharing life with life. For the Chagga, "Sangara" or "Kinyange", for the Baganda " "Akatale" or "Katale" for the Kikuyu. For the Haya "Omujajaro" and for the Ngoni, "Kusoku" for the Sukuma "Igulilu" for the Jaluo "Chiro" etc. Unlike the neoliberal demonisation of the market all these "Sokoni" concept deeply imply a non mutant and non militant reality of shared life.[30]

Last, globalization from below necessarily implies empowering

---

[29] Samuel Kobia, The Courage to Hope p. 72.
[30] World Council of Churches, Theology of Life: A Dossier Geneva, WCC Publications, pp 3-6.

and capacity building for and with the poor. This necessarily implies a new liberating business whereby the poor get disentangled themselves both from within and without.

Globalization of Ethical and Human Values

First, it is true that globalization is inevitable. However, in order to make a socio-economic and ethical difference on human life today it is absolutely necessary to embark on alternative globalization particularly of basic human values. Among others, these include "globalization" of human dignity, trust, peace, justice, sustainability, responsibility freedom, love, solidarity, preservation of life, temperance, care, hope, sympathy, generosity, sacrifice, humanness, fairness and so forth.

Second, currently humanity and society have a huge responsibility to search both for a world ethos and new orientation for a better world. H. Kueng and Angela Rinn-Maurer, (2005) admits that humanity needs a new world ethos ("Weltethos") and orientation ("Orientierung") based on human and ethical values.[31] Indeed, the present claims for the so-called New World Order" particularly by the world's big financial institutions (W.T.O, World Bank, and IMF) need to be replaced by what I consider as "New World Ethos."

Globalization of an African Ontology and Epistemology

On the first place, the capitalist (Western) individualistic view of life economy, wealth and reality is based on this: I think therefore "I am." It has to be replaced by a better vision which is inclusive characterized by relationality and belongingness. As John S. Pobee sums it, "Homo Africanus" cannot simply be satisfied with "a purely materialistic and secular world view.[32]

---

[31] Hans Kueng, Maurer Angela R., Weltethos: Christlich Verstanden (Freiburg: Herder, 2005), See also Hans Kueng, Project Weltethos (München): Piper, 2004) pp. 80-85.

[32] John S. Pobee, Gospel and Culture Pamphlet: West Africa (Geneva: WCC Publications, 1996), 23

Second, the African concepts of "Utu" "Ubuntu" or "Umunthu" and their varied forms, strongly reiterate the typical African spirit and philosophy of humanness, respect for the sanctity of life and dignity. This is particularly achieved by being together not by competition, through the spirit of fraternity, hospitality and mutual love. On its broadest and deepest sense, "Utu" means being humane and considerate with all forms of life, human and non human.

Globalization of Foundational Elements of a Credible Environmental Ethics

First, the human person is to be considered simply as a steward and not the lord of the universe. Responsible stewardship simply means duly serving for the good of humans and non humans.[33]

Second, in the quest for a new environmental ethic, needs to strongly reinstate the basic key elements which act as "instrumentaria" for environmental sustainability. These include *inter alia*, The Golden Rule, (Mt: 22:37-39), the principles of subsidiarity, solidarity, sufficiency and sustainability. These eco-principles are complemented and galvanized by an ensemble of environmental criteria particularly the integral, precautionary, cooperation, savings as well as the main-cause criteria.

Third, we have to globalize a much simpler way of life particularly among the affluent societies world wide. The rich need to live a simple life in order for the poor to simply live. The so-called "Wegwerfgessellschaften" (throw-away societies) need to be replaced by more sustainable earth communities. Hence, inversing the Champagne Glass economy with a better life style and vision. At this juncture, an interreligious approach to a reasonable culture of fasting and temperance could be of great ecological relevance and paradigmatic change.

---

[33] Vatican City, The Call to Justice: The Legacy of Gaudium et Spes 40 Years Later March 16-18th 2005 (Unpublished Papers) p.38.

The Effects of Sin and Evil (Injustices)

On the first place, we have to acknowledge that sin exists. Any type of sin radically destroy the triad relationship between the human person, community and the Creator (God). Human sin transgresses the God-given limits seeking to be like God (See Gen. 3). Admittedly, the current neoliberal ideology of economic globalization in particular thrives on endless economic growth and financial profitability. It ignores and outrightly rejects the material needs of all and particularly the poor.[34]

Second, in biblical parlance, greed is considered as a manifestation of sin. "Everyone is greedy for unjust gain (Jer. 6:13), For I know....how great are your sins you who afflict the righteous, who take a bribe, and push aside the needy in the gate" (Amos 5:12).

Last, from a theological point of view, living under the hardships wrought by economic globalization indicates the gap ("lacuna") on one hand between this earthy life and the future not yet realized life. In brief, it denotes the imperfect nature and character of the material world.

Some Concluding Remarks: Which Way Forward?

In this chapter, I have tried to underpin empirically the intensity and wanton effects of economic globalization both from the African viewpoint and globally. However, a step further beyond these empirical facts was absolutely necessary in order to unveil the deep seated and hidden ideological as well as philosophical behind the forces of contemporary economic globalization. Admittedly, this step is a breakthrough quite crucial especially for a radical change of this current economic paradigm. The last part has tried to testify my hypothesis that, "The business of business is business." This implies humanity and the poor and Africans in particular, cannot avoid the forces of economic globalization. Indeed, today, we are in a sense in the midst of a massivestorm adrift and struggling to astray our socio-

---

[34] Lutheran World Federation, *Engaging Economic Globalization as a Communion* (Geneva: LWF, 2001), 15.

ethical, economic, religious and spiritual values and bearing. Admittedly, there are numerous alternatives. Today, humanity cannot simply stay aloof or resort to flight. Humans regardless of creed, gender and status are called to search and fight for a better world driven with better philosophical visions, worldviews and economic alternatives. The world needs to have better ethical parameters, criteria norms and principles toward a credible economic and environmental global ethics. This is a continuing journey and endeavour with a far bigger picture than ever. At this juncture allow me to conclude this chapter by reinstating again some few key basic issues deemed extremely important.

First, Africans and the poor in particular, need to embark on a revitalization of life giving and life sustaining world views (John 10:10). As Kobia sums it, there "is great value in reconstructing the African traditional philosophy that defined the individual as meaningful only in relation to others. Outside of such interwoven relations, the individual person however materially rich is actually nobody.[35]

Second, the search for fairer world requires inter alia, a true global solidarity built on an authentic global ethics. Among others, reaffirming the intrinsic dignity of every human person and the interconnectedness of all forms of human and nonhuman life. Further, it must entail a paradigmatic shift from the focus on individual wants to social needs, from greed to hospitality, from accumulation to service, from exclusion to inclusion from market fundamentalism and idolatry to agape economy and life. In brief, from self-centredness to a global culture of communion, justice and sharing. Indeed, today, global business and ecological ethos is needed than ever before.

Last, the quest for "better" or "different" economic alternatives remains an absolute necessity. It is a perennial search and ethical project involving all of humanity for better and more just world. Nonetheless, among others African scholars, ethicists, economists, politicians, religion leaders, need to galvanize views and efforts fro a better world. Admittedly, this is not a completed job. It has just began. This is only a first step marking a long and tideous economic and ethical journey.

---

[35] Samuel Kobia, *The Courage to Hope* p.122.

References

African Ecclesial Review Challenge to Preserve Humanity in AFER, Eldoret, *Gaba Publications* October – December 2004 Volume 44, Numbers 5 and 6.

Cortina Adela, Carreras Ignasi "I Buy Therefore I Am" Barcelona, *CJ Booklets*, Vol. 116, 2004.

Cox Harvey, "The Market as God," *The Atlantic Monthly*, March 1999.

Evangelische Kirche von Westfalen, Globalisierung, Bielefeld,-Evangelischer Pressverband fuer Westfalen und Lippe e.v. 2004.

Greider William, *One World, Ready or Not: The Manic Logic of Global Capitalism*, New York; Simon and Schuster 1997.

Kobia Samuel, *The Courage to Hope Geneva*, WCC Publications, 2003.

Krasma Beth (ed) *Thinking Ethics*, London, Profile Books, 2005.

Kueng Hans, Maurer Angela R, *Weltethos: Christlich Verstanden*, Freiburg, Herder 2005.

Levine Robert, *International Herald Tribune*, July 18-19, 1998.

Lutheran World Federation, *Engaging Economic Globalization as a Communion* Geneva, LWF, 2001.

Maria Josep F. Globalisation: "Ah, Yes….. It is Marvellous Excuse for Many Things" Barcelona, *CJ Booklets*, Vol. 100, 2001.

Mkapa, Benjamin W., Address to Officially Open the AMECEA Fourteenth Plenary.

Msafiri Aidan G., The African Ecological Crisis as a Theological and Ethical Challenge: A Case Study in Tanzania (Unpublished PhD Dissertation) Vienna, 2003.

Msafiri Aidan G., *The Church as Family of God Model in African Theology Today*, Scranton The University of Scranton Press, Vol. I, 2002.

Mshana Rogate R., "In Search of A Just Economy" *Alternatives to Economic Globalization*, Geneva, WCC Publications, 2003

Ntagazwa Arcado D., Welcome Statement to the Lake Victoria Environmental Project – Scientific Conference Mwanza 6-10 August 2001.

Pobee John, *Celebrating the Jubilee of the World Council of Churches*, Accra, Assempa Publishers, 1998.

Pontifical Council for Justice and Peace; Compendium of the Social Doctrine of the Church, Vatican City, Libreria Editrice Vaticana, 2004.

Rich Sebastian L, Rich World, Poor World, Sal Terrae Santander 1992.

Schlitt Michael, *Umweltethic: Philosophisch-ethische Reflexionen-Theologische Grundlagen Kriterien*, Paderborn, 1992.

Sindima Harvey in Charles Birch (ed) *et. al.*: *Liberating Life, "Community of Life,"* Maryknoll, New York: Orbis Books, 1990.

Spaemann Robert, *Moralische Grundbegniffe*, Muenchen, Becke Reihe, 1991.

St. Augustine University of Tanzania (SAUT) "Environmentalist Issue" 1 September 2005.

Stueckelberger Christoph, *Global Trade Ethics*, Geneva, WCC Publications, 2002.

The Evangelical Church in Germany, The Common Good and Self-Interest: A Memorandum of the Evangelical Church in Germany, 1991.

The United Republic of Tanzania, The President's office, The Economic Survey 2004, Dar es Salaam 2005.

Vatican City; The Call to Justice; The Legacy of Gandium et Spes 40 Years Later, March 16-18th 2005 (Unpublished Papers).

Victoria Javier, "A Just Economic Order," Barcelona, *CJ Booklets*, 1998.

Wagwe S.M., F.M. Musonda "Local Perspectives on Globalization: The Economic Domain" *Research on Poverty Alleviation*, Dar es Salaam, Mkuki na Nyota Publishers, 2002.

World Council of Churches, Justice, Peace and Creation Team: Alternative Globalisation – Addressing People and Earth (AGAPE) Geneva, WCC Publications, 2005.

World Council of Churches, JPC Team, *Alternative Globalization: Addressing People And Earth*, Geneva, WCC Publications, 2005.

Zulehner Paul M., *Pastoral-theologie, Band 4 Pastorale Futurologie, Duesseldory*, Patmos Verlag, 1990.

Chapter Two

RETHINKING ABOUT THE ROLE OF THE CHURCH ON THE HIV/AIDS AND THE POST ARV CRISES: A TANZANIAN PERSPECTIVE

Abstract

The Church's role particularly in responding to the ever devastating multiple effects ensuing from the HIV/AIDS as well as the post Anti-retroviral (ARV) treatment poses one of the greatest pastoral, ethical, economic familial and societal crises of our times. Admittedly, by her very divine call, mission and vision, the church has a perennial pastoral duty for an integral and holistic salvation liberation of the human person. Among other biblical passages, the following in particular, succinctly reechoes this epistemological and ecclesial truth of the church in all ages: "The spirit of the Lord is upon me, because he has anointed me to preach the good news to the poor. He has sent me to proclaim freedom for the prisoners and recovery of sight for the blind, to release the oppressed, to proclaim the year of the Lord's favour" (Luke 4:18-19).

Unfortunately, hitherto there has been move empirical and mathematical-oriented approach and criteria especially in assessing the demographic impact of the HIV/AIDS pandemic in particular. Truly, these approaches has overlooked the new and unforeseeable of the entire crisis. Today, more than ever before the post ARV treatment challenges in particular, pose new spiritual, ethical, pastoral and psychological dilemmas. These go beyond mere materialistic, demographic and financial quantifications and criteria. Moreover, these new challenges are not only horrendous but they call for urgent and new holistic approaches and solutions, individually, personally, ecclesially, nationally, regionally, ecumenically and globally too.

Consequently, the church and the other ecclesial communities in Tanzania in particular, need to critically rethink about their "traditional" methods and approaches to this pandemic and go step further. Hence, the quest for a radical paradigmatic shift especially in adequately responding to the post ARV drugs and new scenarios as well as the cultural and societal dichotomies and contradictions connected to it. The current new challenge therefore go beyond and they are far much more deeper than governmental standardization, subsidations, NGOs financial aids and the WHO huge donations for ARV therapy and all generic drugs. In brief, there are new pastoral ethical and societal challenges which were not foreseen in the last ten years or fifteen not only by secular and health organizations, but equally by church and ecclesial organizations in Africa, Tanzania in particular. These form the crux of this chapter.

Introduction

Status Quaestionis

The last twenty years has remarkably witnessed significantly ever increased global and local efforts especially in the fight against the HIV/AIDS pandemic. These have in recent years been strengthened particularly by the invention, distribution and even subsidasion of the ARV drugs worldwide. Nonetheless, the war is far from being over. In certain areas things have even worsened. Indeed, the crisis has not been overcome particularly in Africa and Tanzania in particular. Truly, new challenges for instance re-infections of the "resurrected" post ARV treated patients are dramatically and substantially increasing the number of infections especially in Tanzania year by year.

Furthermore, the commodification of the global condom industry and its consequent condomisation of relationships, are faced with massive antagonisms with Christian sexual and marital ethics and religious norms. These pose new unforeseeable ecclesial, socio-ethical and pastoral and ecumenical dilemmas and challenges today and more so tomorrow.

Today, therefore, the church's obligation in rethinking and responding to these new challenges is in conformity to the basic tenets of the Good News especially in providing holistic salvation and care for all and especially the sick, the poor, the marginalized, the suffering, the orphaned, the widowed, the downtrodden etc. On its deepest and strictiest meaning and implication, holistic care "designates complete and integrated response to the needs of a human person ranging from spiritual, physical, psychological, social and material. This care is to be given both to the sick in our communities and those in hospital...."[1]

Justification

Admittedly, the church's role in fighting against the HIV/AIDS pandemic cannot be exaggerated. She has tried to be in the fore front in her holistic ministry of healing as commissioned by Jesus of Nazareth. However, the churches response must always be in the art and manner wishes by her founder "A man with leprosy came to him and begged him on his knees. If you are willing, you can make me clean. Filled with compassion, Jesus reached out his hand and touched the man. I am willing, he said be clean! Immediately the leprosy left him and he was cured." (Mark 1: 40-42). People living with the HIV/AIDS and post ARV treatment in Tanzania are increasing year after year. This necessarily creates new unforeseeable pastoral, ethical as well as societal dilemmas too.

Statistically according to recent estimations and projections package (EPP) developed by the World Health Organization for Tanzania, it is estimated that 1,810,000 people were living with HIV (840,000 males and 960,000 females) at the end of the year 2003.[2] Furthermore, the report goes on affirming that on "the basis of the estimations that only

---

[1] The 15th AMECEA Plenary Assembly Uganda, Responding to the Challenges of HIV/AIDS within the AMECEA Region: A Common Framework of Action 3rd – 11th June 2005 Nairobi, Ruaraka Printing Press pp 15-16.

[2] The United Republic of Tanzania, Ministry of Health, National AIDS Control Programme, HIV/AIDS/STI Surveillance Report Jan-Dec 2003 Report Nr 18., October 2004 p. vii.

1 in 14 AID cases are reported, a total of 187,940 cases are likely to have occurred in the year 2003 alone, females being 98,290 and males 89,650). Today, these numbers have even doubled or tripped. They simply indicate the head of an ice berg. There is need to go beyond these statistical and demographic quantifications and criteria. Quite often they tend to "ignore" or overlook" the deep rooted causes of these crises.

A fresh rethinking and reevaluating would necessarily aims at addressing the deep seated multiple pastoral ethical, theological, epistemological cultural and anthropological truths, benchmarks and criteria. Hence, searching for holistic and permanent answers and solutions beyond just mere statistics. Today, the Christian Churches and ecclesial communities as well as the ecumenical community both individually and collectively, need to take the lead.

The Scope and Structure
In this chapter, I purposefully intend to critically and deeply re-evaluate and rethink and readdress the role of the church re particularly in responding to the dilemmas emerging from the HIV/AIDS crisis, scenarios and more so to the post ARV drug treatment, commodification of condoms giving way to condomization of sexual relationships but also "disposability" of "friendship" the resultant antagonisms and the constant conflicts between sexual ethics and bad cultural beliefs and trends in Tanzania and Africa in general. Hence, going beyond mere mathematical criteria. Indeed, they occasion new and deep pastoral ethical, theological as well as existential challenges to each Christian Church individually and collectively. Chapter one tries to give a focused and brief perspective from a Tanzania perspective and more specifically from a PASADA as a case study. In the Archdiocese of Dar es Salaam, Tanzania PASADA stands for: Pastoral Activities and Services for People with AIDS Dar es Salaam Archdiocese.

As regards its structure, this chapter entails three parts. The first is a brief case study of the PASADA. It intends to be representative of the Catholic Church's response to the HIV/AIDS pandemic especially from a Tanzania African perspective. A brief attempt to particularly underscore the magnitude of the crisis its strengths (excellence) and weaknesses (limitations) will also be made. The second part tries to identify and underpin the real picture beyond the mathematical causes and reasons of this crisis. Hence, breaking the "traditionalistics" and "narrowistic" approaches, prognoses and alternatives. Hence, developing a more holistic deeper and more radicalist approach or paradigm. Among others, there are horrendous and tragic reasons behind this ever decimating monster. These include, the hitherto unforeseeable and unaddressed post ARV treatment dilemmas and scenarios, the deification and commodification of condoms the condomisation of sexual relationships today, the ever conflicting and schizophrenic and antagonistic cultural sexual beliefs, contradicting diametrically opposed to Christian sexual ethics at personal, marital secular, societal, institutional et alii levels.

The last part unveils of relevant anthropological, theological, ethical, ecumenical as well as pastoral perspectives and benchmarks towards more credible solutions which have so far not been searched for. In Tanzania in particular and Africa in general. At this juncture therefore it is worthy and extremely necessary to ask and ponder on such critical and deep questions such as: Why is the number of HIV/AIDS victims not decreasing despite all church's state, private and secular efforts? Are the churches aware of the new dangers and challenges emerging from the post-ARV new infections and reinfections within and outside marital life? What is behind the condomization of relationships today? What can churches do individually and collectively? Truly, there are no ready made answers to these several other questions. All in all, we need to have the courage not only to hope for the seemingly hopeless, but to decide and act now personally, ecclesially, ecumenically, collectively and globally too.

Empirical Part

The HIV/AIDS And Post ARV Treatment Challenges Today: A PASADA Perspective in Tanzania

Its Magnitude: A Brief Tanzanian National Real Picture
According to a recent HIV/AIDS Indicator Survey (Nov. 2005) developed by the Tanzania Commission for AIDS, TACAIDS, 7% of Tanzanian adults aged between 15-49 years are infected with HIV. The prevalence is higher among women 8% than among men 6%. The intensity varies from one region to another. Regions with notably highest HIV prevalence and cases are Mbeya with (14%), Iringa (13%) and Dar es Salaam (11%).[3] The magnitude of HIV/AIDS as well as the new challenges arising from and ever devastating massive new infections and re-infections of the ARV treated patients goes beyond any statistical quantifications. This is an undisputable fact. Let us now stream line our focus to the PASADA paradigm and approach.

A PASADA Case Study and Perspective

Origins and Pastoral Vision And Functions
The name "PASADA", is an abbreviation for "Pastoral Activities and Services for People with AIDS Dar es Salaam Archdiocese." This is a catholic owned non governmental organization. Its premises are located near to the Chang'ombe Catholic Church in Temeke district in Dar es Salaam region. As a service-oriented and with a non governmental and non profit making status, PASADA started to operate in the year 1992 as a concrete response in providing holistic, medical, pastoral and counseling services to people living with HIV/AIDS in Dar es Salaam and its vicinity particularly from coastal region. PASADA is one of the best examples and pilot studies of the Catholic Church's response to the HIV/AIDS challenges. Admittedly, there are similar

---

[3] Tanzania Commission for AIDS (TACAIDS) 2003-2004 Dar es Salaam 2005 p.69

church based diocesan and non diocesan health department in all the catholic diocese of Tanzania under the Tanzania Episcopal Conference. All these are trying to offer immense pastoral, medical, socio-economic and spiritual services. PASADA is one of the best and most successful example.[4]

PASADA Philosophy

In responding to its mission and vision, Pasada devotes itself to provide the highest quality of service particularly in showing love, sympathy, understanding to the people living with HIV/AIDS in the archdiocese of Dar es Salaam. However, special attention and priority is given to the poorest of the poor, the disadvantaged and the needy. Quality and holistic services based on the ethics of justice and solidarity with the suffering are deemed to be an absolute necessity and priority.[5] Jovin Riziki Tesha, "Ripoti kwa Mkuu wa Mkoa wa Dar es Salaam katika kuadhimisha siku ya Ukimwi Duniani 1.12.2005, iliyokabidhiwa rasmi tarehe 20.2.2006 page 3.

Personnel

Pasada has both employed and voluntary workers. Latest statistics indicate that there are 130 fully employed workers and 300 voluntary activists.[6] Despite of being a non profit service oriented organization, PASADA has always been getting donations and funds to cater for its administrative, pastoral and medical costs from governmental as well as from non governmental organizations within and outside the country.[7]

---

[4] Interview with Mr. Jovin Riziki Tesha research and advocacy officer of PASADA, Dar
[5] Jovin Riziki Tesha, "Ripoti kwa Mkuu wa Mkoa wa Dar es Salaam katika kuadhimisha siku ya Ukimwi Duniani 1.12.2005, iliyokabidhiwa rasmi tarehe 20.2.2006 pg.3.
[6] Jovin Riziki Tesha, "Ripoti kwa Mkuu wa Mkoa" (2006) p.3.
[7] Interview with Jovin Riziki Tesha, Dar 10.10.2006.

Target Groups
PASADA offers its services freely to everyone in need regardless of his or her faith tradition, ethnic group, status, and gender. For example recent statistics indicate that the target groups (2006) include 49.7% Moslems, 50% Christians and 0.3% others.[8] Up to the end of the year 2005, the number of HIV/AIDS victims getting different services from Pasada was 15,200 apart from orphans who amounted to about 4,100.

Services Given by PASADA: Strength (Excellence)
As a non profit making church organization, PASADA offers its invaluable pastoral oriented and holistic, medical and psychological services particularly in the following major areas.

Pastoral Care and Holistic Counselling
This service is freely availed to clients who voluntary would like to know about the status of their health in case they have been infected by the HIV virus. Clients and interested persons from the archdiocese of Dar es Salaam and its vicinity get pastoral counselling services from PASADA's based health centres and dispensaries. The basic goal of pastoral care and counselling is to curb new infections and re-infections and to specifically inculcate hope, positive lifevision and capacity building to people living with HIV/AIDS.

PASADA HIV/AIDS Testing Centres
Currently (2006)[9] PASADA offers HIV/AIDS testing opportunities at the following dispensaries under the Health Department of the Archdiocese of Dar es Salaam. These are: Ukonga Dispensary, Msimbazi Dispensary, Tegeta Dispensary, Kawe Dispensary,

---

[8] Jovin Riziki Tesha "Ripoti kwa Mkuu wa Mkoa" (2006) p. 3.
[9] Jovini Riziki Tesha, "Ripoti kwa Mkuu wa Mkoa" p.4.

Chang'ombe Dispensary, Mbagala Dispensary, Yombo Dispensary, Luguruni Dispensary, Mbweni Dispensary, Manzese Dispensary and Sinza Dispensary. Beside these, PASADA has extended such services to Vikindu, Kilimahewa, Mkuranga as well as to Kibiti dispensaries in the coastal region.

Voluntary Testing: VT Services

Latest findings (2006) indicate that approximately about 1500 people every month go for the HIV tests. Pasada offers counselling before and after these tests. Counselling services are both holistic and sustainable. It is argued that, due an increase in the number of the HIV infections annually, people who go for voluntary tests are now in thousands. These meet every first Thursday in month for extra medical and psychological activities. Among others these include small self-reliant economic projects and activities such as small businesses, gardening activities, handwork, sewing, etc. In collaboration with Caritas Dar es Salaam, PASADA has tremendously improved the economic and life conditions of several interested clients especially in providing loans with relatively reasonable lower interest rates.[10]

Furthermore, PASADA provides its pastoral care and counselling activities known as "play therapy" to children (orphans) whose parents have died of HIV/AIDS or ST live with the pandemic or children who lack enough time for testing treatment physical exercise. This includes emotional support, (companionship, counselling) material support food, cloth and support with schooling.

Some Challenges and Weaknesses: Limitations

Among others, PASADA has recently identified the following as the major problems particularly facing its pastoral and counselling endeavours and ministry.

---

[10] Jovini Riziki Tesha "Ripoti kwa Mkuu wa Mkoa" (2006).

Today, there is a notably large increase in the number of people and clients seeking for pre-testing counselling, testing and post-testing services. PASADA personnel as well as the available financial, human and medical facilities cannot cater for all these.

Emergence of new infection and re-infections particularly arising from "resurrected" clients and patients who have considerably regained good health from ARV therapy and therefore sexually quite active.

Quite often Pastoral Care and Counseling activities are greatly being affected due to the long distances between the centres and the amount of time needed by counsellors to reach clients. Hence, hampering both the effectiveness and efficiency of this programme.

It has also been observed that, unlike adult clients and patients, children and orphans do not get sufficient care and time especially in addressing their psychological, physical and medical and pastoral needs.

As it will be shown later, PASADA and Tanzania in particular and Africa in general, is being faced with unforeseable ever new and complex post ARV scenarios and coupled with conflicting socio-cultural, economic, anthropological and religious beliefs, traditions as well as world views. These have been worsened by the current geo-cultural process known as the condomisation of human sexuality and relationships." Hence, the need today to critically rethink and re-evaluate the hitherto approaches especially in identifying their weaknesses (limitations) and eventually searching towards more credible "formulae" methodologies permanent solutions and hopes.

Socio-ethical Part

Rethinking Beyond Demographic and Statistical Approaches to The HIV/AIDS Crisis in Tanzania (Africa) Today

At this juncture, let us now try to critically rethink and therefore go beyond the normal "mathematically oriented approaches" which have hitherto been employed to fight against this pandemic. Undoubtedly, the search for a more holistic and effective approaches is a conditio sine qua non for eradication of HIV/AIDS world wide and Africa (Tanzania) in particular. Among others, the following critical scenarios in particular and facts substantially constitute the major dilemmas and facts making the eradication of HIV/AIDS a nightmare particularly in Tanzania including patients under PASADA too.

The Unforeseeable Post ARV Treatment Dilemmas

The invention of the ARV therapy to HIV patients has brought not only hopes, but also new social, ethical, economic and pastoral challenges. Observation indicates that, a great percentage of patients who receive to get the ARV therapy with balanced diet manage to survive and live longer than usually expected. Hence, regaining not only good health, but also sexual desires. In other words, they become sexually active. This category of people includes either couples who one of the partners is infected or both. It includes also infected or non infected widowers, widows, singles, orphans, children, etc. Indeed, their number unlike in the former days is remarkably increasing. Consequently, giving rise to higher risks and possibilities not only of infections, but more so re-infections both to the not yet infected as well as to the already infected persons. Truly, prior to the therapies ARV, chances for a "prolonged survival" were quite narrow and minimum. Today, every month and year the number of people living with HIV/AIDS especially in Sub-Saharan Africa and Tanzania in particular is notably increasing. Hence, increasing also not only the hopes for survival of the victims, but risks for more infections and re-infections. Hence, the hopes and new challenges inherent in the post ARV therapy. This gives us one of the hints why the number of HIV/AIDS is on the increase despite the ARV therapies today! Such dilemmic scenarios and risks have undoubtedly increased the socio-ethical, pastoral, and religious economic needs and all round multifaceted issues connected with the HIV/AIDS crisis. Conclusively, as Peter Poit once commented: "I want to emphasize that Africa should not make the same mistakes as the west did when ARV's became available. The result was terrifying an increase in infection"[11]

---

[11] Paul Chummar C., "On `Inculturated Theological Ethics in Africa" Unpublished Paper May 2006, CUEA Nairobi p. 2.

Condomisation and Disposability of Relationships

By condomisation, I mean the present day geo-sexual trends and culture of massive production, advertising and distribution of different types of male and female condoms world wide, in Africa and (Tanzania) in particular as if they were the surest and most efficient means of eradicating HIV/AIDS. In Tanzania for instance the "Salama" "Rough Rider" the "Dume" condoms and other generic names are vivid examples.

Ethically, the end cannot justify the means. Unethical means cannot give way to a good and dignified end. Moreover, this runs the dangers of reductionism, social nihilism, despair and instrumentalisation of human ratio, free will and conduct. In this vein of thought, Emmanuel Katongole (2005), strongly argues any credible solutions against HIV/AIDS in Africa without paying attention to the broader socio-ideological, political and material situations in Africa[12] is both illogical and cynical.

Second, from a socio-ethical view point, Katongole goes on asserting that, "any attempt to isolate AIDS from this wider context and simply reduce the issue to one of a "viral infection" is not only misleading, but it is an ideological trap whose effect is to perpetuate the myth of Africans as incurably promiscuous. This in turn provides a self-justifying promotion for condomisation as the only way to curb the spread of the disease.

Third, the process of condomisation of Africa in general and Tanzania in particular has its foundations and "inner logic" from the present day neo-liberal global consumerist culture and throw away society. By their very nature, condoms are disposable commodities like disposable razors, Coca-Cola, Fanta, Sprite, cans, Ketch up/tomato, plastic bottles, plastic bags available in all supermarkets and shopping malls globally, lunch boxes and containers, etc. Today, all these and

---

[12] Emmanuel M. Katongole, A Future for Africa Scranton: The University of Scranton Press, (2005) 41-42.

several others are constantly being succumbed into a post modern turbo culture of disposability. A throw away society. Worse still, this culture has eventually crossed material and tangible phenomena into "love" relationships "friendships", partnerships" non-tangible aspects of human life. Consequently, strictly speaking the issue here "is not just about the convenience of disposable condoms, but more importantly, it is about the popularization of a certain form of sexual activity, one detached from any serious attachment or stable commitment."[13] Conversely, condomisation promotes a highly destructive ideological belief and world view of considering both sex and sex partner(s) as essentially disposable, superficial, temporary and detached from any serious responsibility and commitment. It "deifies" that, condom hence making it a "guaranter" of human telos and destiny. In short, an ethical problem necessarily needs an ethical solution and not simply a material solution.

The "Abstinence", Be Faithful or "Use a Condom" (ABC) Ideology, and Its Weaknesses

Today, many people both literate and illiterate, rich and the poor world wide and Tanzania in particular simply believe and subscribe to the unsatiable dictates, formulae and new whims and promises of the media junkies. The power of advertisements is enormous especially in promoting a global erotic culture characterized by condoms, multiplicity of contraceptives, drugs, like the "viagra" for enhancing sexual vitality, erotic television programs, internet pages, pornographic cyber culture and wanton accessibility to pornographic material.

Due to these huge obstacles in particular, most of the efforts to personalize chaste and good sexual behaviour among world's populace

---

[13] Emmanuel M. Katongole A Future for Africa p.43.

and youth in particular simply become nightmare. Worst still, the three options highly advertised, as the optimal solution to the HIV/AIDS ABC (Abstain, Be Faithful or Use a Condom) are per se contradictory, illogical and they do not carry the same weight. Indeed, research and human experience show that among many humans "Abstinence" and "Being Faithful" seem to be quite difficult. Truly, these need inter alia a strong will power, discipline and sacrifice. To use a condom seems to be the easiest and "cheapest" alternative to many sexually active persons, youth as well as adults. Consequently, almost 98% of all sexually active youth would opt to it!

Ethically, at this juncture, a triad of "three seemingly equal alternatives" cannot be accepted and therefore justified as if its three components carry the same weight and seriousness. The first two necessarily need ethical determination, sacrifice, moral maturity, responsibility, stability, permanency, honesty, discipline, modesty, integrity and virtue. Naturally, this unveils the great weakness inherent in the ABC advert as the "most suitable formula and panacea to eradicate HIV/AIDS especially in Tanzania and Africa in general. Why? People tend to choose easiest solutions and answers in life.

Critical and Contradictory Sexual Models, Beliefs and Convictions

Up to now, there have been more focus and emphasis particularly to Western oriented models, formulae, approaches, by most of the anti HIV/AIDS activists. Quite often, the deeper concrete socio-cultural, economic and life contexts and situations especially in Africa (Tanzania) behind HIV infections have either been ignored or overlooked. Consequently, giving rise to perennial contradictory situations, dichotomies and scenarios hard hitting "homo Africanus", than the rest of human beings elsewhere. Let us now identify these four major ever contradicting scenarios.

Four Contradicting Scenarios as Developed by Msafiri Aidan

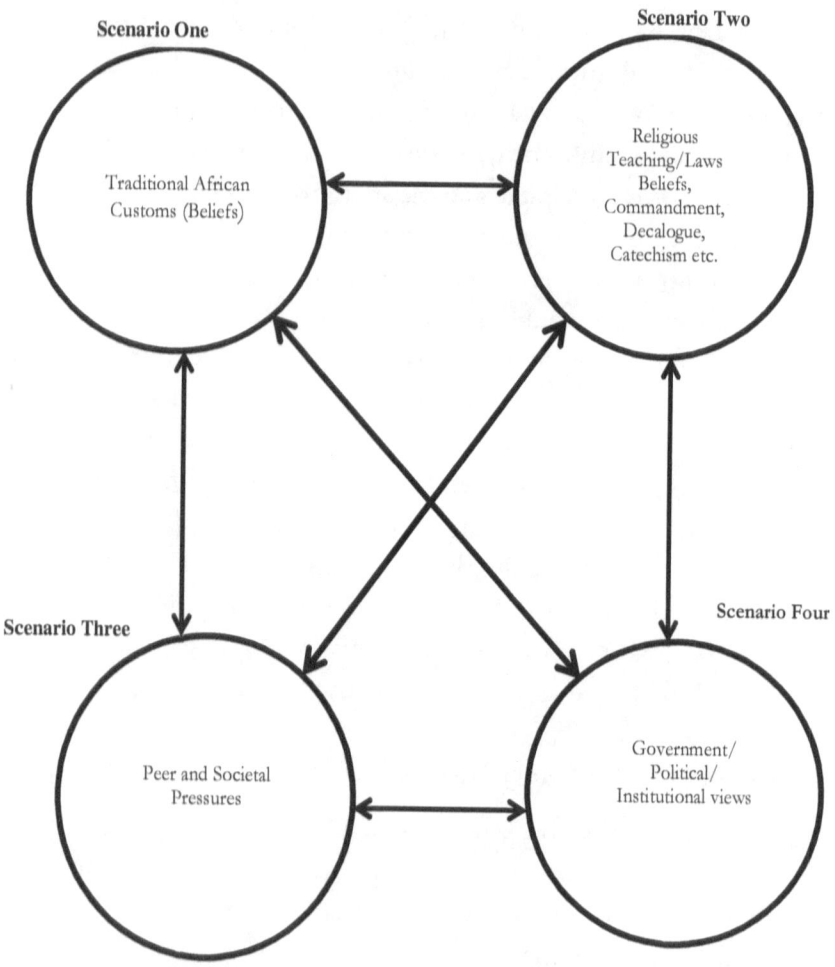

Copyright: *msafiriaidan@2006*

Explanation and Concrete Examples

In all these four scenarios, there are constant dichotomies and clashes of values. Examples:

Scenario One Against the Scenario Two
In a Christian family, a wife in a patrilineal society (e.g. the Chagga) is married and both are Christian and has given birth to 10 children all being girls. The "traditional Chagga" package and worldview hitherto allows and encourages inheritance to male children only. She herself requests her husband to "get" a male heir through extra-marital sexual activity. However, this is diametrically opposed to scenario two. Refer the sixth (Ex. 20:14) and the ninth (Ex. 20:17) precepts of the Decalogue. Such an existential "value clash" easily leads to HIV/AIDS infections, arising from such atangonistic contexts and "Sitz im Leben."

Scenario Three Against Scenario Two
A Christian lady or woman for a example who is a secretary to certain director or politician could end up getting HIV infection inspite her good Christian moral upbringing when her fellow women workers who have been laid redundant from their jobs, who in turn ill "convince" her to have extra-marital sexual affairs in order to retain her job. Note the inherent tension here.

Scenario Four Against Scenario Two
Government or media oriented policies e.g. promotion and use of Condom are diametrically opposed Christian morals. These open the greater risks for HIV/AIDS infections. Other similar tensions could easily be identified. Conclusively, contradictory situations clash in ethico-religious cultural economic world views, happen as indicated in the ever opposing arrows above. Hence, giving way to further HIV infections especially within the African (Tanzania) life situations. Worst still, there are confused mind sets and contradicting solutions to the same problems both within and outside church and secular circles.

A Growing Tanzanian (African) Culture of Despair, Hopelessness and Orientationlessness
Today, many young people are very desperate. They lack the deeper meaning of life. Among other reasons, object poverty as well as a

culture of laziness in Tanzania in particular are main causes. It is not uncommon today, if one asks a girl living either in the village or urban areas "Una malengo gani ya maisha" (What are your goals in life), she would immediately reply, "Sina malengo yoyote maishani" ("I do not have any goals in life") "Sina kazi" ("I am unemployed") "Sina mtaji" ("I do not have any capital to launch a project"), etc. In such situations, there are enormous risks for such a girl or girls to simply succumb into unethical activities especially sexual promiscuity. Hence, increasing the number of HIV infections in Tanzania in particular.

Having identified all these, let us try to make a way forward especially by rethinking on our hitherto theological, ethical, pastoral, religious and ecumenical models and view and benchmarks and suggest better and more credible interdisciplinary, approaches and solutions against the HIV/AIDS arise amidst such wanton antagonisms and conflicting scenarios particularly in Tanzania today and tomorrow.

Concluding Theses and Benchmarks: Which Way Forward?

Rethinking Theologically

What can Theologians in Africa do? Today amidst more than ever before, African theologians, scholars, priests, pastors and "periti" need to rethink particularly about the following benchmarks and truths.

Reconstruction of a Theology of Relationships
Relationships have their origins and dynamics in the triune God. All that God does in and with humans and creation is directed towards relationships. Hence, it is an opportune moment or "Kairos" for African theologians to rethink again especially on our tasks of doing theology to promote human relationships and search for alternative ways of theologizing in general and Tanzania in particular.

Reconstruction of a Credible Theology of Life
African theologians and Tanzanian in particular need to critically rethink and reconstruct a credible theology of life amidst and in the contexts

of the HIV/AIDS and the post ARV crises. These dilemmas need creative and well reflected and systematized responses and solutions especially from theologians, Christian Churches, and ecclesial communities. Thus, re-bringing life in abundance (John 10:10).

As Samwel Kobia (2003) aptly puts it: "We are called to transform this tragedy by linking life to a moral cosmology as the means to reclaim the intrinsic value of being in the World"[14]

Rethinking About Sin Repentance and Forgiveness
Indeed, in our freedom as humans, it is possible either to accept or reject relationship with God and act as if it does not exist. Ontologically, the distortion of being in relationship[15] or creature vis-à-vis creator is called sin. Actions or relationships which harm others or the rest of creation are in se sinful. In short, there is need today to rethink particularly on the theological and spiritual reconstruction on the imperative need for true repentance or metanoia. This would underscore a proper reaction to a perception of what sin is, and its multiple effects in terms of pain suffering and misery especially in the HIV/AIDS and the post ARV crises today.

Rethinking About Divine Punishment
Tragically, some theologians, church leaders and Christian churches have identified the HIV/AIDS with divine punishment. Today, there is need to rethink and critically reevaluate this position. Truly, a God who forgives will not necessarily by His very nature be concerned to punish. There are neither biblical accounts of creation nor metaphysical understanding of God attributing Him the desires for punishment.[16]

From the New Testament perspective, "when Jesus to link sin with disaster, he refused utterly: "No I tell you" (Luke 13.3 cfr. John 9:1-3).

---

[14] Samwel Kobia, The Courage to Hope (Geneva: WCC Publications, 2003) 178.
[15] WCC Study Document Facing AIDS: The Challenge, The Churches' Response (Geneva: WCC Publications, 2004) 25.
[16] Ibid, p.27

It may happen in private spirituality that the experience of HIV/AIDS may lead a person to repent of his or her own actions, as indeed other suffering may have this effect....It is important to distinguish between punishment for an action and the consequences of an action...To speak of an event as "punishment" from God, however, attributes to God a requirement for retribution"[17]

Reconstruction of A Theology of Compassion Healing, Hope and Solidarity
Today, theology especially in Africa (Tanzania) needs to reconsider and remake Christian Churches and ecclesial communities as real "loci" (places) and sanctuaries of life for those living, suffering and dying from HIV/AIDS. Among others, special focus need to be directed in the following.

Avoiding the culture of "kunyanyapaa" (stigmatization) those infected with HIV/AIDS. Quite often, stigma is created not only due to fear, but also by ignorance of the facts or denial of the basic facts. Nothing could be more cruel to those infected than to believe that HIV is not the cause of AIDS. The science and research establishments of both the first and third worlds concur that the HIV virus is the virus that causes AIDS"[18]

The churches' holistic ministry of healing, needs to be reconstructed. For long this has been considered an integral part and parcel of the proclamation of the Good News. Jesus cured every disease and every sickness (Mt 9.35). Later on, he commissioned his disciples to do the same. This is reechoed in the New Testament's heading narratives (Lk 9:1-2, Mk 16:18, Acts 3:1-8, Lk 10:25-37, Mt 10:8, Lk 4:2-3, Lk 5:17 etc).

---

[17] Ibid p.27
[18] Njongonkulu Ndungane, A World With a Human Face, (Geneva: WCC Publication; 2003) 59-60.

Truly, holistic healing or life in abundance has a bodily dimension. Nonetheless, it necessarily entails a transcendental salvific aspect. Consequently, holistic healing can occur at the expense of the body or even at the expense of an individual life. Jesus' death is the most vivid example and highest experience to us all (See John 15:13, Isa. 53:4, Mt 8:17, 1 Pet. 2:24).[19]

In short, "the cross makes us aware that the healing ministry of the church cannot simply consist in working to prolong life or to promote body concepts that favour strong, not mutilated, perfectly healthy bodies (and most probably those that are young and beautiful). Instead, the very task of this ministry is to reinstate the "God-likeness" to all men and women, children and adults, rich and poor, the healthy and sick. It is to enable as many people as possible to live their lives in such a way that others can recognize the image of the living God in them......"[20]

In a nutshell, therefore to live the churches ministry of holistic healing is necessarily to witness to the corporeality of salvation. This is nicely echoed in the words of Tertullian, the early African theologian when he re-emphasized that the "body is the pivot of salvation"[21] Here comes also a theology of suffering and death, hope and resurrection (Rom 8:38-39).

Rethinking and Reconstruction of Ethics for Africa (Tanzania)

Today, African ethicists in particular, need to embark on this urgent project. The following areas need special and urgent review in particular. It is imperative that a new culture of understanding integral human sexuality be reconstructed. Sexuality is a "precious gift from God our Creator to every man and woman. We are therefore called to honor it,

---

[19] Lutheran World Federation, Study Book for the Healing of the World, LWT Tenth Assembly, Winnipeg Canada, LWF (Geneva: 2002) 188.

[20] Ibid p.188

[21] E. Evans, Tertullian's Treatise on the Resurrection (London: SPCK, 1960) 26.

respect it, and use it according to God's commandment and teaching of the church"[22]

The indigenous African traditional ethic and ethos regarding human sexuality need to be revisited and re-emphasized especially in the context of the HIV/AIDS and the post ARV therapy crises. Hence, sexual encounter should necessarily be seen as being communal and not only being a self-centred and individualistic highest value. All dimensions however, are crucial and relevant.

Together with its immense potential especially in promoting richness of intimacy and joy, sexuality exposes people in Tanzania (Africa) particular to the risks of HIV infections. Therefore, there is urgent need to avoid misuse of sexuality whereby people do simply ignore their personal responsibility. Both personal and ecclesial ethics need to be revisited.

Today, more than ever before, African ethicists and scholars in particular, need to rethink and reconstruct new pedagocial methods especially in implementing healthy Christian ethical principles, visions, norms and ethos. This will help to eradicate the present day infectious culture and behaviour among "homo Africani."

Rethinking Ecumenically and Pastorally: What can African Churches Do? Indeed, the search for credible and holistic solutions to the HIV/AIDS and the post ARV crises belong to the very mission and vision of the ecumenical and inter faith organ locally, nationally and globally. Why?

Today, the church should again realize and acknowledge that in order to adequately respond to the ever changing many facets of the HIV/AIDS and the post ARV crises, it is absolutely necessary to work together as the body of Christ and as a true community of healing, compassion and solidarity. Truly, an effective and well organized networking within the ecumenical body will necessarily bring the most effective results.

---

[22] AFER AMECEA 15th Plenary: Responding to the Challenges of HIV/AIDS within the AMECEA Region, (Eldoret: Gaba Publications, December 2005 Vol. 47 – Number 4 & March 2006, Vol. 48 – Number 1) p 387.

From an ecclesiological view point, the ecumenical community needs to remind itself of this altruism that, by proclaiming the Good News of Jesus of Nazareth, the churches 'espouse "the message of social, individual, national and international wholeness. For the church, all people, regardless of their gender, class, ethnicity, race, age, religion are created in God's image and life itself is God's will for humankind and creation as a whole (Gen.1-2)"[23]

In short, the ecumenical body is constantly being called to express its availability and concern to the sick, the suffering, the desperate, the bereaved, the orphaned and widowed. As the body of Christ, the ecumenical community should necessarily see itself as the body of Christ which is deeply infected and affected because its physical members (1 Cor 13:9-10) too suffer and die! Hence, the church needs also healing.

Reconstruction of Capacity Building Against the HIV/AIDS Pandemic and Post ARV Crises

Today, there is great and urgent need particularly, in building Church's capacity in responding to these crises. Among others, this should be endowed with the following key tenets: The need to learn more especially in conducting interdisciplinary research in different fields particularly related to the HIV/AIDS crises.

Theological Curricula particularly in the seminaries and higher institutes of learning, (e.g. Colleges, Universities) need to be reviewed, revisited and re-improved particularly in responding to HIV/AIDS as a whole.

The Role of Small Christian Communities in Africa particularly in responding to these crises need to be reconsidered

Indeed, Christian Communities should not and cannot estrange themselves from the real needs and sufferings of the people. Hence,

---

[23] Musa W. Dube (ed) HIV/AIDS and the Curriculum, (Geneva: WCC Publications, 2003) p.155.

they need to be truly empowered particularly in the establishment of viable programmes and support initiatives aimed at reducing the risks, opportunities, spread and the multiple impacts of the HIV/AIDS and the post ARV dilemmas.

Lastly, today there is urgent need for the church in Africa in general and Tanzania in particular, to rethink about her competence especially in terms of her material, human, spiritual, pastoral, ethical, medical all round competence particularly in responding to these crises. Among others, the PASADA model is one of the commendable models trying to timely and adequately respond to these new challenges and dilemmas. Admittedly, there is still a long way to go. There are neither ready-made nor short cut answers. However, together and individually too we have the obligation to rethink, review and reconstruct our socio-ethical, cultural and religious world views, norms, principles ethos for a better Tanzania (Africa) with a human face. As "homo Africani" we strongly believe "I am because we are." Consequently the need to show true solidarity particularly with our fellow sisters, brother, children, parents, friends, neighbours, fellow humans suffering and dying from HIV/AIDS. God bless Tanzania, God bless Africa.

References

AFER, AMECEA 15th Plenary: Responding To The Challenge of HIV/AIDS Within The AMECEA Region, Eldoret, Gaba Publications, December 2005, Vol.47 – Number 4 & March 2006 Vol. 48, Number 1.

Chummar Paul C., "On Inculturated Theological Ethics in Africa" (Unpublished Paper), CUEA Nairobi, May 2006.

Dube W. Musa, (ed), HIV/AI DS And The Curriculum, Geneva; WCC Publications, 2003.

Evans E, Tertullian's Treatise On The Resurrection, London, SPCU, 1960.

Katongole Emmanuel, A Future For Africa, Scranton, The University of Scranton, The University of Scranton Press 2005.

Kobia Samwel, The Courage To Hope, Geneva, WCC, Publications, 2003.

Lutheran World Federation, Study Book for The Heading of the World LWF Tenth Assembly, Winnipeg, Canada LWF Geneva 2002.

Ndungane Njongonkulu, A World With A Human Face, Geneva, WCC Publications, 2003.

Tanzania Commission For AIDS 2003-2004 (TACAIDS), Dar es Salaam 2005.

Tesha Jovin Riziki "Ripoti Kwa Mkuu wa Mkoa wa Dar es Salaam Katika Kuadhimisha Siku ya Ukimwi Duniani 1.12.2005, iliyokabidhiwa 20.2.2006, (Unpublished Paper) Dar es Salaam.

The 15th AMECEA Plenary Assembly Uganda, Responding to the Challenges of HIV/AIDS within the AMECEA Region: A Common Framework of Action 3rd – 11th June 2005, Nairobi Ruaraka Printing Press.

The United Republic of Tanzania, Ministry of Health, National AIDS Control Programme HIV/AIDS/STI Surveillance Report Jan-Dec 2003, Report Nr 18, October Dar es Salaam 2004.

WCC Study Document, *Facing AIDS: The Challenge, The Churches' Response* Geneva, WCC Publications 2004.

Chapter Three

NATURAL LAW ETHICS AND CONSUMERISM TODAY

Abstract

This chapter tries to make a profound and critical analysis particularly of the ever growing and worsening antagonism between current consumer culture or ideology and the ultimate human telos.

First, it underscores the philosophico-existential and epistemological truth that the greatest neurosis of our times is the ever increasing and insatiable passion and craving by humans for the temporary material goods and ends. That is, a persistent and constant human inclination towards "having" rather than "being". Among others, the ever growing "Mall Culture" particularly in North America, Europe and Asia (China) is a clear example.

Second, from an ethico-philosophical viewpoint in particular, this treachery and inner stimulus for the excessive and irrational production and consumption of temporary material goods, is contrary to the basic tenets and goals of natural law ethics on material goods and things. The view and teaching of natural law ethics particularly on material goods and human life is necessarily oriented and based on the ultimate telos. That is true and transcendent happiness. Hence avoiding the addiction of possession centrism and immediate gratification "hit et nunc." Philosophically, this originates from the wanton economic and human developments especially brought by "homo faber" and "homo oeconumicus" in the post-modern era, whereby everything is based on this triad, production, marketing and consumption.

Third, the entire corpus and logic of contemporary consumerist ideology is based on a wrong philosophical, epistemological and anthropological world views that "I consume therefore I am" or "I buy, therefore I am". This is diametrically opposed to the dictum. "I think therefore I am". Indeed, consumerism focuses its immediate attention and concern particularly on immediate cosmic sensual satisfaction and gratification. Truly this does not necessarily lead to true happiness or a better (or higher) quality of life.

Fourth, from the perspective of practical reason, this dichotomy particularly between consumerism on one hand and normative ethical truths and values necessarily on the other, alludes to the epistemological truths of what really makes human beings truly happy. At this juncture, the role and place of human reason is of paramount importance particularly in giving human beings a deeper meaning and telos of material things. Hence, getting out of this crisis as propounded by the irrationalistic human superfluous production and insatiable consumption stimuli and ideologies today.

Lastly, through proper use of natural law ethics and human reason, humans need to free and eventually transform their consumption and egoistic ideologies into an eschatological and transcendental way as the ultimate telos of material things embued with ultimate meaning and true happiness. In brief, the crisis of consumerism is more of a philosophical and ideological problem than economic. Consequently, the need to underpin the transcendental as well as epistemological and ethical truths and values in today's consumerist world.

Prolegomena

The Issue at Stake

The entire global community today is profoundly being driven by ever growing insatiable stimuli for limitless consumerist ideologies and goals. More than ever before, humanity is witnessing a radicalist geo-philosophical and geo-ideological shift from the Cartesian, "I think, therefore I am" to "I consume, therefore I am". It unfolds and manifests strongly in today's consumerist life styles globally. Adela Cortina and Ignas Carreras (2004) succinctly make the following observation: "it is no longer a question of goods that are basic and necessary but rather the current trend is in buying superfluous unnecessary goods"[1] Admittedly, behind such a powerful post-modern consumerism, there is an increasingly ever growing and rapidly spreading powerful contagious consumerist philosophy and ideology worldwide.

The Cambridge Encyclopedia defines consumerism as the "promotion of policies aimed at regulating the standards of manufacturers and sellers in the interests of buyers. The stimulus may come from government, through legislation, from an industry itself

---

[1] Adela Cortina, Carrera Ignas, "I Buy Therefore I Am" (Barcelona: CJ Booklets, 2004, Vol 116) p.4.

through setting up codes of practice, or from consumer pressure groups."[2] Today, this consumerist ideology is not only becoming commonplace but it is taking ideological global proportions as well as expressions politically, economically, socially, technologically, genetically, environmentally and even religiously.

Justification

From a philosophical point of view, the present day global consumerism is diametrically opposed both to fundamental moral principles and truths of natural law ethics and truths intrinsic in every human person by his or her Creator. Consumerism occasions one of obscuring and conflicting areas particularly with regard to natural moral truths. As one of the present day every growing socio-ethical, theological and philosophical challenges and dilemmas, consumerism unveils clearly in the "lacuna" (gap) especially between ethics on one hand and human rationality.

Joseph Ratzinger (now Pope Benedict XVI) prior to his nomination, aptly underscores this dichotomy through the following observation: "The present rupture between ratio functionalis of the natural sciences and the ratio ethical, leads to a divergence between the empirical sciences on one hand and philosophical and theology on the other…"[3] In other words, this has led to what he calls "the dictatorship of relativism." Among others, such a contemporary irrationalistic and subjectiristic world view and stance has dramatically changed the perception of the human good in almost every area of life. And in this case in particular in the destructive and irrational consumerist culture

---

[2] David Crystal (ed), The Cambridge Encyclopedia, (Cambridge, Cambridge University Press, 2000) S.V. "consumerism."
[3] Joseph Ratzinger, Letter on Natural Law, Ethics, Congregation Pro Doctrina Fidei, Vatican City November 5, 2004 p.1.

and attitudes. Consequently, the ever growing destructive materialistic, economic and radicalist and subjectiristic consumerist stimuli in particular, necessarily call for a rethinking of basic and undisputable truths and values inherent especially in the natural law for more sustainable, rational and responsible consumption patterns especially in the fields of modern technology, politics, economics, communications (media) environment to mention a few.

Scope, Vision and Structure

This chapter specifically searches for more reasonable future sensitive and sustainable consumption patterns based on fundamental truths of natural law ethics, philosophy and theology in particular. Such a new rethinking and rediscovery is of urgent and paramount relevance particularly in readdressing and curbing consumerism its destructive socio-economic, technological, cultural, spiritual, environmental and philosophical consequences today. Hence, our vision is geared towards a true socio-ethical and philosophical paradigmatic shift based on unchangeable eternal truths and ethical attitudes encapsulated in natural law ethics.

This chapter entails three major parts. In the first part, an attempt is made to unveil some anthropologico-ideological and philosophical signposts, contours and world views especially pertaining to consumerism today. The approach is profoundly interdisciplinary and broadspectrum in nature. The second part tries identify and re-accentuate the key philosophical foundations, dimensions, relevance and truths of natural law ethics particularly in underlining the illogical nature of the phenomenon of consumerism. The last part tries to entails a number of important theses integrating and encapsulating among others, key socio-ethical, philosophical, theological environmental and technological truths and benchmarks towards more balanced, rational, sustainable consumption patterns not only for today but more so in the future. Hence, natural law based approach towards the creation (production) distribution and "telos" (end) of human and non-human goods and services in contradistinction to the present day ever growing "throw away" consumerist culture world wide.

Undoubtedly, this quest is everybody's business and concern. It is not an easy or one day task. It is a perennial process. Nonetheless, among others, African scholars, philosophers, theologians, ethicists, experts, economists and every person of good will in particular have a special role and duty in the entire quest or process of bridging the ever growing "lacuna" (gap) and antagonism between ethico-philosophical truths on one hand, and utilitarianistic, relativistic ideologies of natural sciences today. Indeed, we need a globalization of concern and proper vision in proactively addressing global divisions, antagonisms and challenges particularly ensuing from destructive and nihilistic consumerist life-styles locally and globally. We need to think globally and act locally.

Some Anthropologico-Philosophical and Ideological Roots, Signposts and World Views for Consumerism Today

Fundamentally, the anthropology and philosophico-anthropological background of modern consumerism is based on "a persistent orientation towards more "having" rather than "being"... This confuses the criteria for correctly distinguishing new and higher forms of satisfying needs from artificial needs which hinder the formation of a mature personality."[4]

On its deepest and broadest meaning, the post-modern consumerist culture and edifice, entails *inter alia*, anthropologico-ideological, philosophical, economic, environmental, technological religious as well as cultural dimensions backgrounds and overtones. The following deserve special attention and concern in particular.

---

[4] John Paul II, Encyclical Letter, Centesimus Annus 36: AAS 83 (1991) 839.

The "Methods" and "Principles" of Consumerism: Some Nine Anthropologico-Ideological Views and Beliefs.

"The-You-Need-More-Than-One-Fashion" (Design) Method
This principle insatiably drives humans to have and consume more and more from the same commodity or service. Today for example a person "needs" more than one type of PC's, TV screens, shampoos, perfumes, cars, etc.

The Once-and-Then-Throw-Away" Principle
In this world view, humans tend to use or consume some good or services only once. This belief and principle has given rise to the present-day throw away society. ("Wegwerfengesselschaft")

The Principle of Limitless/Endless – Technological Development
This accentuates technological messianism and breakthrough whereby huge and unpredictable technical developments particularly in the fields of ICT, biotechnology, genetics, nanotechnology, bites, atoms, genes, information, and communications system, trade to mention some, simply become the end and not the mean any more.

The Constant-Commodity-Transformation-And-Betterment Principle
The ideology or myth behind this world view is specifically the present-day inner longing and quest for an endless re-modifications, renovations, restructuring and redesigning of consumer goods and services worldwide. It perpetuates wanton consumerist life-styles and patterns.

The "Changing-of-Old Models-Method-And-Tactic's" Principle
This anthropological world view which propagates the belief that the old models cannot be repaired. Consequently, the need to endless designs and ever new technological advancement and innovative

models. Indeed, this encourages unnecessary consumption patterns especially in the fields of science, technology, production and services globally.

The "Complication's System-Method" (Principle)

As an anthropological and ideological stance, this principle tries to persuade and convince consumers (humans) today, that the product is just too complicated that one "necessarily" and "immediately" needs a totally new product after using it. This consumerist "credo" drive humans to always adhere to ever new product and innovations.

The Credit Card System and Culture

The post-modern consumerist society is increasingly and notably being characterized by the triumph and hegemony of the credit card system. Today, the use of physical cash or money is simply being discouraged. People both in the developed and developing world are simply carrying different banking, financial, insurance, transport (hire a car, plane, etc) club and communications cards, worldwide express cards, the american express card, the eurocard, mastercard, dinner club card, regus card, travelex card, world teleconnect card etc. The "credit card culture" (ccc) is becoming commonplace globally. In the banking world, the "ATM" cards are increasingly becoming commonplace even in the remotest parts of Africa, Tanzania, Kenya etc.

The "Ponda-Mali-Kufa-Kwaja" Principle ("Enjoy Life Now, Death-Is-Near" Principle)

Indeed, this philosophico-ideological worldview, is a powerful force particularly for the consumerist hedonist culture today. It legitimizes both irrational and unsustainable consumption patterns whereby the rationality shifts from "I eat in order to live" to "I live in order to eat," or "I buy therefore I am" or "I consume therefore I am."

The Hegemony (Sovereignty) of Children's -Markets-And-Goods-Principle

In this case, today gigantic supermarkets and shopping malls specialized in children's goods, strongly convince children and parents to absolutely purchase different consumer goods for children (e.g. toys, play stations, candies, books, etc.) even if when parents do not want. In this way parents are "forced" to supply their children with more and more material pleasures and materials. This ideology is largely contributing to unnecessary as well as irrational and unsustainable consumerist life-styles worldwide.[5]

Utilitarianism and Consumerist Culture

Today, human sciences in particular, indicate that, utilitarian preferences and stimuli in particular originate from human craving to consume.[6] Truly, economists and production experts prefer the ideology and "more is better." This ideologico-philosophical world view, attributes "happiness" and satisfaction to proximate rather than to ultimate goods. Further, it propagates a destructive cultural and ideological corruption which is more dangerous than the atom bomb. It propagates a utilitarianistic creed, that, "You are what you consume."[7] That is the right "High-definition T.V screen," the right car, the right mobile phone, the right deodorant, the right shampoo, shirt, necktie, house etc. People believe that their personality and respect depends on the type of car or commodity they own or consume. Everything is marketing and consumption. Its logic, can aptly be summarized in this present-day consumerist "formula: "I believe in profit, super profit and all the profits" regardless of whichever negative socio-ethical, human or philosophical truths and values are transgressed. Admittedly, more is not always good, or rational.

---

[5] Matthias Horx, "Wie Wir Leben Werden" (Frankfurt/New York: Campus Verlag, 2006) 159
[6] Vatican City, The Call To Justice, The Legacy of Gaudium, Et Spes 40 years Later, March 16-18, 2005 p.147.
[7] Antonie Wessels, Secularized Europe (Geneva: WCC Publications, 1996) 25.

The Neo-Liberatist Argument and Consumerism

Today, neoliberalism is greatly contributing to wanton consumerist patterns, attitudes and life-styles, Javier Victoria (1992) observes that, "one of the basic facets of neoliberalism is the aspect of fanaticism and fundamentalism."[8] According to the present day neoliberal argument, the consumer is his master. Ironically, the consumer is simply considered as the only social agent who makes his or her decisions in a rational, and single-minded manner.

Further, this ideological stance claims that the consumer is fully informed on all the seemingly possible choices and consequences of what he consumes. The consumer has a veto vote: "I want this commodity, not that one." In short, the businesses which truly work best are only those that receive the highest number of public votes. Consequently, giving consumers what they "want" and not what they "need."

The Unlimited Economic and Technological Growth Argument and Consumerism

Fundamentally, the Western ideological belief and argument particularly in the quest for endless economic and technological progress, is fuelling the insatiable stimuli and propensity for more and more consumption. This has far reaching negative economic and technological consequences and implications. The present day Western view of post-modern production simply means the myth of unlimited expansion, production, possession and acquisition.

Among others, the present-day mushrooming of giant shopping malls particularly in North America, Europe and Asia (China) clearly indicates a major geo-economic and consumption shift today. As it has recently been observed, in China for example "80 percent of

---

[8] Javier Victoria, A Just Economic Order, CJ Booklets (Barcelona: 1998) 10.

shoppers walk to the mall.... In some megacities, including New Delhi, Nairobi and Rio, urban sprawl has flung customers into outlying neighborhoods, many of which spring up around brand – new shopping centers..."[9]

Indeed, consumerism tries to convince the consumer that it is absolutely "necessary" to have more and more and even more from everything. Among others, this includes, two houses, three cars, at least four refrigerators, seven pieces of digital radios, MP3 and DVD players, twelve suits and the "litany" goes on and on. The consumer, will strongly believe that without possessing at least a number of commodities or reach a certain life standard, he will simply be regarded as already living at the "sub-standard" or poverty level.[10]

The consumerist world today considers the world, economy and technology to be only for the service of humans and not vice versa. This has given way to the exaltation of the geo-anthropocentric and evolutionistic belief that the human person is simply considered as "homo faber" (producer).

Its origins come mainly from the wanton intellectual as well as technological developments from "homo habilis" to "homo erectus" to "homo sapiens" to "homo technicus" to "homo digitalicus" to "homo oeconomicus" and eventually "homo cybericus." These developments have substantially increased consumption life-styles and mega trends worldwide.

Environmental (Ecological) Destruction and Consumerism

Today, irrational and unsustainable global resource consumption patterns are exerting imminent pressure and threat particularly on humans and the earth as a whole. Among other areas, the ever looming environmental consumption terror is particularly evidenced in present

---

[9] Newsweek, "Mall World: American-Style Shopping Complexes, December 5, 2005 page 27.
[10] Matthias Horz, "Wie Wir Leben Werden" page 159.

day eco-crises of global warming, depletion of natural resources and loss of biodiversity (soil fauna and soil flora) to mention a few. Recently, it has been claimed that the world "will lose 30 to 70 percent of the world's biodiversity in a time span of 20 to 30 years."[11]

From an Indian perspective for example, it is estimated that by the year "2017, India will be a water stressed country, because the per capital water availability will be as low as 1600 cubic meters. Ground water exploitation is increasing rapidly (both for qualitative and quantitative reasons) resulting in the decline of water table in most places...Again, according to official estimates in 1980, 56.6 percent of the land suffered from environmental degradation, especially water and wind erosion..."[12]

As far as global warming is concerned, it has strongly been remarked that if "global warming is to be held to less than 0.1 degrees centigrade per decade, U.S. per capita carbon dioxide emissions must drop from 19.5 tons today to 6.6 tons by the year 2010 and 1.7 tons by the year 2030.... And the consumption of natural resources overall will require reductions of 60 to 90 percent. Yet the UN Earth Summit (Rio), Population Summit (Cairo), and Social Development Summit (Copenhagen) treaties were virtually devoid of targets in consumption levels, an omission that marks Agenda 21 as well."[13]

In brief, today the gravity and intensity of global environmental degradation is reaching catastrophic proportions. As one eco-futurist expert recently observed at the Second International European Futurist Conference in Lucern, (Nov. 2006) in which I too participated, today,

---

[11] World Council of Churches, Alternative Globalization Addressing Peoples and Earth, (AGAPE), (Geneva, WCC Publications, 2005) p.9.

[12] Aruna Gnanadason, Listern to the Women, Listen to the Earth (Geneva: WCC Publications, Risk Books,2005) pp 7-8.

[13] Larry L. Rasmussen, Earth Community, Earth Ethics, (Geneva: WCC Publications, 1996)p.152.

humanity needs two more planets like the mother earth in order to satisfy our needs for sanitary water, air, food, etc. Future prognosis shows that in the year 2050, air and water will be sold at quite high prices. And the future wars or conflicts will result from humanity's struggle for water and not oil.

Commodification of Religious and Liturgical Feasts and Celebrations

Today, more than ever before, there is a growing global trend to consider and make religious occasions and celebrations a major source of business enterprising and financial super profits. Among others, the Christian celebration of Christmas provides a concrete example. As regards Christmas, one is not surprised today to see huge advertisements and transactions of Christmas carols, songs, decorations, candles, symbol, trees, cribs, vestments, cards, St. Nicholaus (Father Christmas) candies, lights, etc. In Europe it takes place five months before 25th December. That is in July every year.

This is not uncommon particularly in the present-day huge Euro-American shopping centers, supermarkets, malls, shopping streets, etc. Such items, goods and commodities are strongly being advertised by the powerful modern media junkies almost in every language world wide. Truly, every year the situation gets worse and worse and sooner or later it will get out of control.

Parallel to that, today, there is a very strong global religious trend for commodification of new religious communities, organizations and movement. In some mega cities particularly in North America, someone has recently observed that one comes across a Christian Church called "The Church of Christ." However, two hundred meters on the next street or avenue, one sees another religious building written "The Very Church of Christ". On the next street, there comes another Church named "The Very Very Church of Christ." Indeed, the word "Very" keeps on increasing reaching even 32 times in the same city! Is this phenomenon not alluding to a post-modern commodification of religion tainted with consumerist and utilitarian motives and goals?

The Post-Modern Communication's Technology and Consumerism

Today, there is a quantum leap and breakthrough particularly in the fields of media, information technology and particularly the indomitable power of advertising globally. The later for example plays a great role and place especially in fuelling wanton consumerism. Today, highly developed advertising techniques persuade humans to believe that happiness and joy "come through fancy new clothes, more expensive cars, the latest fashions and increasingly sophisticated gadgets."[14]

Ideologically, the logic behind the advertising agencies is to always create "dissatisfied customers." Negatively, massive financial profits simply depend on the so-called "the virtue of qualities like wastefulness, self-indulgence and artificial obsolescence."[15]

Undoubtedly, global corporations and media junkies, simply create an insatiable craving, lust and stimuli for ever more audio-visual consumption. As Jean-Nicolas Bazin and Jerome Cottin observe; "Many adverts for software or computer programmes show us the consumer Adam or Eve, giving to the temptation pick the forbidden fruit: the limits have been crossed, the prohibition superseded, the contract broken...."[16]

Worse still, particularly on a much broader global picture as far as consumerism in communications system today is concerned, statistics

---

[14] Hans, Ucko, The Jubilee Challenge: Utopia or Possibility (Geneva: WCC Publications, 1997) p.118.
[15] Quoted in George F. Will, "The Politics of Soulcraft" Newsweek, 13 May 1996 p.158.
[16] Jean-Nicolas Bazin and Jerome Cottin, Virtual Christianity, (Geneva: WCC Publications, Risk Books, 2004)p.100.

indicate that "a New York reader consumes more paper each Sunday than an African in a year, only 17 countries have a gross national product greater than total expenditure on advertising in the USA; four agencies control 96 percent of the entire flow of news in the world."[17]

In short, there is huge pollution of information world wide and particularly in the developed countries. The tricks lies in the following, either new virtual needs are created, they become infinite and unquenchable or advertising agencies simply succumb in deploying "the most sophisticated combinations of beautiful women, gorgeous colours and splendid soundtracks to guarantee that self-indulgence and instant gratification replace frugality and simplicity…"[18] Truly, the great founders of the great religions, (Jesus of Nazareth, Buddha, Mohamed etc) did not give people what they "wanted" but what they "needed." Today, there is urgent need to critically rethink on the necessary and key differences between "wants" and "needs."

At this juncture, let us now move to part two and try to identify and underpin the meaning content and relevance of basic natural law ethics as credible and inspiring foundations towards credible and sustainable solutions.

Natural Law Ethics (Ratio Ethica) and Consumerism: Quest for Credible Solutions

Fundamentally, the basic truths and tenets inherent in natural law ethics are diametrically opposed to both irrational and unsustainable consumerism. Let us now try to briefly explore the meaning and underline and also revisit its foundational principles as illuminating and relevant aspects against consumerism today.

---

[17] S.T. Kwame Baofo, (ed) Communication and Culture: African Perspectives (Nairobi: WACC-Africa, 1989) p.vi.
[18] Hans Ucko, The Jubilee Challenge p.118.

Natural Law: Meaning

According to St. Thomas Aquinas, natural law (lex naturalis) is described as the participation of the rational creature in it the eternal law of God, insofar as it is relevant and knowable to humans.[19] Natural law is the same in all humans and "it has regard primarily to those things which are necessary to human nature. From the fact that the natural law is founded on human nature itself it follows that it cannot be changed, since human nature remains fundamentally the same, and it is the same for all. It can be added to, in the sense that precepts useful for human life can be promulgated by divine law and human law…"[20]

Cristina L. Traina considers natural law as being "about ends; it is human, self-conscious participation in this divine comprehensive plan. Thus, it directs human beings to the same sorts of ends as other members of the natural world – for instance, physical and communal flourishing – but it also distinguishes human beings from those other members by steering us to the transcendent, eschatological perfection of love and knowledge."[21]

Undoubtedly, this view encapsulates and reechoes the basic traits and components of natural law and natural law ethics a whole. Consequently, natural law ethics ensues from the edifice of natural law as a practical philosophical, human and ethical ability and illumination for a creative transformation of human life and the world. Against the challenges of post-modern consumerism, natural law ethics underpins and shows the rational ethical approach.

---

[19] Thomas Aquinas Summa Theologiae 1.2. 92.2.
[20] Frederick Copleston, A History of Philosophy, (London: Burns Oates & Washbourne Ltd, 1954) p.407.
[21] Dieter T. Hessel, Ruether Rosemary R, (eds) Christianity And Ecology (Cambridge, Massachusetts, 2000)p.251.

Natural Law: Its Content and Relevance

It Promotes Good and Avoids Evil

According to St. Thomas Aquinas, the fist basic tenet of natural law is to do good and avoid evil.[22] Further, he considers it as truly being self-evident. That means, at least "it is a reasonable statement of faith – unprovable yet a necessary assumption for doing ethics as an appropriate response to encounter with value."[23] Conversely it accentuates the Kantian ethical theory of categorical imperative which asserts that "always do good and avoid evil." This entails positive prima facie duties and virtues both individually, collectively and communally.

It is a Ground of Human and Environmental Rights

Human and environmental rights constitute fundamental and necessary conditions of the natural law edifice. Indeed, as necessary conditions for human well-being and dignity, such rights are universal and egalitarian in nature. Their extension embraces the following categories in particular: biophysical and economic needs; physical security; spiritual and moral autonomy; mental and cultural development, full and equal participation in defining and shaping the common good, social ground rules for fair and equal consideration; environmental security as an extension of biophysical needs and common good itself as the ensemble of conditions' that favors the realization of individual in community the total constellation of rights fairly distributed, balanced and blended.[24]

---

[22] Thomas Aquinas Summa Theoligiae 1.2.94.2
[23] Daniel C. Maguire, Fargnoli Nocholas, On Moral Grounds: The Art/Science of Ethics (New York, Cross and Press 1991)pp 34-35, 94-95.
[24] John Finnis, Natural Law and Natural Rights, (Oxford; Clarendon Press, 1980) p.154-156, 214-218.

Protection of the Common Good as a Human Good

This is an extremely necessary and integral aspect of the natural law ethics. On its broadest meaning, the principle or doctrine of common good contains and affirms that "many goods essential to integral human flourishing are goods that can be accomplished only collectively, that benefit the whole society when they are in place, to which everyone has a duty to contribute, that everyone has a right to enjoy and whose damage deserves correction – coercive if necessary. Classically, the common good is a human good, the product of human rational activity."[25]

The Teleologico-Transendental (Eschatological) Dimensions

On its most practical sense, natural law (ethics) implies fulfilling temporal ends in such a way that coheres with teleologico-transcendental goods. Hence, "natural-law, human reason-subsists in delicate relationships with the laws of nature – the physical workings of beings and systems that must be respected for the sake of flourishing."[26]

From an ecological point of view, natural law ethics orients and motivates humans to use their reasoning and creative powers to shape and reshape themselves and their environment within the physical and biological limits as well as within the ultimate human telos.[27]

It contains the Totality of Universal Dictates of Right Reason

According to St. Thomas Aquinas, natural law is the summation of the universalistic dictates of right reason particularly concerning the good of nature which needs to be pursued. Further, the evil in human's

---

[25] Dieter T. Hessel Ruether Rosemary R, (eds) Christianity and Ecology p.254.
[26] Ibid pp 251 - 252.
[27] Ibid p. 252.

nature ought to be shunned. For him, it is only through the light and help of reason and freedom humans could arrive at these dictates.[28]

In another treatise on the content and role of natural law the Angelic Doctor succinctly observes that natural law "is nothing other than the light of intellect infused within us by God. Thanks to this, we know what must be done and what must be avoided. This light or this law has been given by God to creation."[29]

In Veritatis Splendor, John Paul II underscores both the role of human freedom, will and reason in human life and ethical conduct. He maintains that the "exercise of freedom implies a reference to a natural moral law, of a universal character, that precedes and unites all rights and duties."[30]

Last, natural law, plays a significantly major role in uniting humanity, common principles and in promoting unity in diversity and global solidarity through an interdisciplinary, inter-religious dialogue and the culture of tolerance worldwide. Hence, paving the way towards a true and responsible "christian" humanism, global citizenship and fellowship.

Let us now try to identify some concluding benchmarks and views in attempting to bridge the "lacuna" (gap) epitomized between the first part and the second part of this paper. That is, the ever increasing rapture between the autonomy and dictatorship of natural sciences ("ratio functionalis") on one hand, and rational ethical truths ("ratio ethica") on the other. These will be encapsulated in a number of ten concluding theses and principles of practical ethical reflection and conduct vis-à-vis the ever worsening crisis of consumerism today.

---

[28] Frederick Copleston, A History of Philosophy, Vol II. Ibid p.409.
[29] St. Thomas Aquinas, In Duo Praecepta Caritatis et in Decem Legis Praecepta Expositio. C1.
[30] John Paul II, Encyclical Letter Veritatis Splendor 61: AAS 85 (1993), 1181-1182.

Rethinking About The Role of Ratio Ethical Against Consumerism: Some Concluding Ten Theses

First Thesis

Today, more than ever before, the unforeseable and ever growing destructive consequences wrought be consumerism, challenge the entire human family, especially to critically, rethink, revisit, redefine and reorient its consumption patterns, life-styles and cultures worldwide.

Consequently, changing the current destructive consumerist worldviews of "having more is better" to "being is better", the "I consume/buy, therefore I am" to "I am therefore I think and "I am because we are."

Second Thesis

There is need to strongly reaffirm the anthropologico-theological truth and fact that human beings are created in the image and likeness of God (Imago Dei). Hence, reiterating the unique dignity and intrinsic worth endowed on each and every human person. As a consequence of this, every human person carries a special duty as a co-servant, co-creater and responsible steward especially in the care, service and solidarity with fellow humans and the rest of the created world. Hence, emphasizing on the paradigmatic shift from commodity to dignity.

Third Thesis

The western myth of unlimited growth and technological messianism humans today need to avoid irrational resource, material production and over consumption attitudes which instrumentalise creation as a mere object and end of human interests. Thus, curbing both depletion of unrenewable and limited global resources. New technologies need to be reassessed and ethically evaluated. They are not value free.

Thesis Four

There is need to strongly reaffirm the principles of charity (love) sustainability, natural law, retinity, sufficiency, community, personality and subsidiarity as foundational principles against consumerism today. Truly, humans need to seriously rethink about the future of both humans and non human species and the rest of creation. The motivating principle should be the "Golden Rule" or "Principle" that is the true love of God and neighbour (Mt. 22:37-39).

Thesis Five

Today, there is great and urgent need especially in redefining the special role of universities, higher institutes of learning, scholars in all walks of life particularly in bridging the yawning gap between knowledge and practice, the ideal and the actual, ethics and consumerism, truth and technological breakthrough etc. The ever growing irrational and unethical trend of massive fragmentation of knowledge and ethics need to be readdressed. We need a reintegration of ethics and knowledge.

Thesis Six

The rediscovery of virtue ethics especially prudence, temperance and moderation in particular, is an extremely essential condition for a better and more rational and disciplined use of created goods. Hence, achieving balance in life. Indeed, such virtues could help humans today rectify and re-orient sub-rational passions and stimuli aggravated by consumerism today. Further, the virtue of justice too, endorses, the "suum cuique" principle. That is, "to each and everyone his/her due."

Thesis Seven

Today's global media communications networks need to readdress the dictatorship of manufactures which encourages more consumption their ability to manipulate, to "seduce" set "the tone", "the agenda" for both hybrid cultures which perpetuate more consumption. In turn this would re-address the current ever growing destructive media-based consumerist trends of commodification of life, sex, love etc. Such present day media dictatorship and hegemony therefore per se opposed to human ratio, freedom of choice and dignity.

Thesis Eight

In promoting unity in diversity, and global solidarity especially in promoting rational consumption life-style, the role of natural law ethics is of paramount importance. Among others, it provides deep insights and vision of living together as a community of life on the earth which in turn promotes the "fiesta de la vita" (the feast of life) among all living and non-living beings.

Thesis Nine

Fased with the idolatry and myth of consumerism which is diametrically opposed to ratio ethica and ratio humana, today humanity needs to embark on an alternative model of globalization. That is, globalization of concern (consciousness) and non addictive behaviours in particular. This entails a global fight against the worship of the idol of consumerism.

Tenth Thesis

Humans need to admit that true and ultimate happiness does not consist in the material possessions, worldly pleasure, utilitarianism, or hedonism, but in the transcendental end, the higher meaning of humanity and creation as a whole. We need to return to this philosophico-theological and eschalological altruism and belief.

Conclusion

Having surveyed and analysed the entire philosophico-anthropological and ethical challenges linked with the consumerism today, few but absolutely necessary truths and observations in particular, need to be reaffirmed.

First, today, more than ever before there is great need to revisit and rethink particularly about the indispensable place and role of natural law ethics against the insatiable and stimuli and tragic consequences of consumerism.

Second, among others, African universities, scholars, "periti" the secular as well as ecclesiastical communities and the ecumenical family in particular, need to critically re-examine the idol and edifice of consumerism today and search for the way forward for better alternatives and paradigma based on ratio ethica.

Third, it is an epistemological, philosophical and theological truth that true and ultimate happiness does not consist in "having" but in "being". Consequently, the need to radically transform the current irrational consumption patterns locally, nationally and globally.

Fourth, better, rational and sustainable consumption life-styles need to start the process of bridging ratio ethica and ratio functionalis and search for an authentic critique of the current dictatorship of relativism. All these are quite crucial steps especially in our quest for a total transformation and change of the consumerist culture symptomatic in every aspect of socio-ethical, economic, cultural, environmental political, religious life today world wide.

Truly, while advocating such a paradigm shift, it must be clear to everyone that, the entire quest requires among other things enormous effort for alternatives credible resistance, global solidarity, unconditional affirmation of life, true vision, focus and determination in particular. We can make the difference for a true transformation and change. Let us start now.

References

Alternative Globalization Addressing People and Earth, AGAPE, Geneva: WCC Publications, 2005.

Aquinas Thomas, In Duo Praecepta Caritatis et in Decem Legis Praecepta Expositio, CI.

Aquinas, Thomas, Summa Theologiae, 1.2.92.2

Baofo Kwame S. (ed), *Communication and Culture: African Perspectives*, Nairobi: WACC-Africa, 1989.

Bazin, Jean N., Jerome Cottin, *Virtual Christianity*, WCC Publications, Risk Books, 2004.

Copleston Frederick, *A History of Philosophy*, London, Burns Oates & Washbourne Ltd., 1954.

Cortina Adela, Carrera Ignas, *I Buy Therefore I am*, Barcelona: CJ Booklets, 2004.

Crystal David (ed.), *The Cambridge Encyclopedia*, Cambridge, Cambridge University Press, 2000.

Finnis John, *Natural Law and Natural Rights*, Oxford, Clarendon Press, 1980.

Gnanadason Aruna, *Listen to the Women, Listen to the Earth*, Geneva, WCC Publications, Risk Books, 2005.

Hessel Dieter T., Rosemary Ruether R., (eds) Christianity and Ecology, Cambridge, Massachussetts, 2000.

Horx, Matthias, *Wie Wir Leben Werden*, Frankfurt/New York, Campus Verlag, 2006.

Maguire Daniel C., Nicolas Fargnoli, *On Moral Grounds: The Art/Science of Ethics*, New York, Crossroad Press, 1991.

Newsweek, "Mall World: American – Style Shopping Complexes," December 5, 2005.

Paul John II, Encyclical Letter Centesimus Annus 36: AAS 83, 1991.

Paul John II, Encyclical Letter Veritatis Splendor 61: AAS 85, 1993.

Rasmussen Larry L., *Earth Community, Earth Ethics*, Geneva: WCC Publications, 1996.

Ratzinger Joseph, *Letter on Natural Law Ethics Congregatio Pro Doctrina Fidei*, Vatican City: November 2004.

Ucko Hans, *The Jubilee Challenge: Utopia or Possibility*, Geneva, WCC Publications, 1997.

Victoria, Javier, *A Just Economic Order*, CJ Booklets, (Barcelona, 1998.

Wessels Antonie, *Secularized Europe*, Geneva, WCC Publications, 1996.

Chapter Four

WOMEN AND THE UNFAIR DISTRIBUTION OF RESOURCES AND WEALTH IN TANZANIA: SEARCHING FOR DEEPER AND TRANSFORMATIVE SOLUTIONS AND ALTERNATIVES

Introduction

Aim

The colourful and gorgeous celebrations and presentations of academic papers on Women's Day occasion a very crucial moment of deep appreciation to all humans and particularly to women. It calls all of us to express thanks to all women particularly as important stakeholders and promoters of human dignity, life values, justice, equity and care takers of life especially at the "Bottom of the Pyramid" (BOP). Please a big applause to all women!

Truly, as women and scholars in particular, we need to go deeper and beyond such celebrations which do not give women their rightful place and opportunities especially in education and eventually in the ownership of wealth, resources, economic planning and leadership roles. From a Tanzania viewpoint in particular, women have for decades if not centuries being excluded and denied of the fundamental human rights, both theoretically and practically.

It is therefore, the right and absolutely necessary for all women and men in academic as well as all people of good will today to critically rethink and re-examine critically particularly as regards the deeper causes behind these socio-economic educational, and political inequalities. Who are behind these injustices? Who are the worst enemies of the women? Some will say men, culture, etc. A broader and deeper view shows that very often women are the worst enemies of fellow women (Refer the song: *"Duniani Kuna Watu na Viatu"* By Nyota Ndogo, Mombasa).

First, in this chapter, I want to show through facts and figures immense contribution of women in economic activities in particular.

Second, I envisage to unveil through the deep-seated root causes and enemies of women particularly from Tanzania perspective. The crux of this problem is from this vicious situation. Indeed, without giving first priority to women's education which necessarily starts the day care schools, primary schools, secondary to colleges and universities. We cannot promote or talk about socio-economic, justice and gender equity. The last will try to give practical deeper solutions and alternatives as a way forward. Let us now, briefly give a statement of the problem is question and the justification of this presentation.

Statement of the Problem: What is the Issue at Stake?

From the demographic point of view Tanzania has approximately a population of about 36.7 million people. Out of this almost 55% are women and 45% are men. According to recent research findings 88% of the Tanzanian population is engaged in agricultural activities lives in rural area. Women constitute the majority of this working population in the agricultural sector working almost for 10-16 hours a day.[1] Inspite of being the major producers of both food, services and cash crops, they are not the major beneficiaries of the remuneration or profit from this sector. Worse still, in most of the Tanzanian households ⅔ of all work is performed by women. This includes market production, child care, cooking cleaning, taking care of the old; sick, disabled as well voluntary religious and community work.[2] Unfortunately, these women's multiple economic roles go unpaid, unrecognized and unrecorded. But

---

[1] African Development Bank BD/IF/2008/50.
[2] Athena, K. Peratta A Caring Economy Geneva, WCC Publications, 2005 p.18.

they are the least rewarded segment! To make things still worse, 90% of the 125 ethnic groups in Tanzania are patrilineal societies. These deny women of their basic human rights particularly the right to own control resources to educational opportunities inspite of (women) being the major drivers of economic development in Tanzania. Again, these and other discrimitory scenarios present a real and concrete problem to be examined and solved especially by women academicians today.

In short, it is true that women have become endless victims of massive human rights violations particularly in the rights to own private property just remuneration,[3] as well their right to plan and manage economically productive projects. Women experience marginalization inspite being a very important segment at the BOP (Bottom of the Pyramid) productions and developmental activities.

Justification

The underlying reasons for this chapter is, there must be something radically and deeply wrong particularly at the familial societal, community, regional and national level which perpetuate these wanton socio-economic injustices instead of promoting true holistic and transformative development of women. This entails especially their right to own and share economic resources and opportunities as a whole.

Beyond doubt, true transformative education, foresight culture, competence, and entrepreneurial skills to mention a few, are necessary conditions for a way forward today. Let us now embark on part one and try to identify the invaluable and massive contribution of women in socio-economic activities in Tanzania on one hand and how the are systemically as well as systematically being deprived of their rights to own and manage resources and wealth as a whole.

---

[3] Aruna Gnanadason, Kanyoro Musimbi (eds) Women Violence and Non-Violent Change Geneva, WCC Publications 1996 pp 30-32.

Lastly, this chapter will try to make a concrete road map of concrete deeper solutions and alternatives for a true change. Hence, going beyond mere celebrations of women's day each year.

Some Socio-economic, Gender Injustices in Tanzania: Facts and Figures/Cheks and Balances

Gender Discrimination in the Access and Control over Resources and Employment Opportunities: Unfair Distribution of Resources

Gender ownership, control and access to employment opportunities in Tanzania are concerned, indicate that, women are largely denied of these fundamental rights. Access and control over resources necessarily includes economic and productive resources particularly land, livestock, employment, credit to mention a few. It entails also political and human resources such as proper education, health, decision making, leadership roles, participation to mention a few.

The Information Labour Force Survey 2000/2001 claims that in Tanzania "84% of the total workforce is in agriculture which produces 47.5% of the GNP. Mean monthly income from agriculture activities for women is 8,232…Women in agriculture work an average of 10-14 hours. Men work 7-8 hours a day…"[4]

Beside these, the patriarchal dominated culture characteristic in most of the ethnic tribes in Tanzania, denies women to the right to own land, livestock and capital. In many tribes e.g. the Chagga, land is only inherited by the male children. This is diametrically opposed to the United Nations Universal Declaration of Human Rights, the 1986 Declaration on the Right to development, as well as the 1993 Second World Conference on Human Rights held in Vienna, Austria.

---

[4] African Development Bank, Tanzania-Multi Sector Country Gender Profile 2005 p.9.

Unequal Employment Chances Amidst Higher Women Economic Productivity
Research findings show that the formal wage sector is only about 8.6% of total employment.[5] This is predominantly constituted of male workers. The rest about 91.4% includes the informal and unskilled sector is largely in agriculture and household activities and services whereby women constitute about 86% of its working force. The agricultural sector contributes 49% of Tanzanian's GDP. In agriculture, women use between 10-14 hours each day for preparing land by hand hoes not tractors, sowing, weeding, harvesting, transporting crops, threshing and storage! Is this not gross gender discrimination and exploitation? There must be something radically wrong especially the familial and grass root levels. That is at what C.K. Prahalad (2006), calls: "The Bottom of the Pyramid" (BOP).

Unequal Opportunities (Chances) for Education and School Enrolment
From the educational point of view, checks and balances indicate that, inspite being greater in population and at the centre of economic activities and production, right from the day care centres to the university levels, women are given fewer and lesser chances. It is said that 76.5%, of girls reach standard 5, and only 59% of girls manage to finish their primary education in Tanzania.[6] The percentages for boys each year are far much higher!

Educational inequalities start from the Bottom of the Pyramid (BOP) upwards. Enrolments at the University levels e.g. at SAUT, UDSM, Mzumbe, Sokoine Universities express the same sad scenarios. Of course, lower numbers of girls at the primary and secondary schools cannot miraculously change to higher numbers. And eventually even in the employment and formal sector in particular.

Statistics for the 2007/2008 enrolment of girls at SAUT in different faculties as an example.

---

[5] African Development Bank 2005/50 p.16.
[6] World Development Indicators (2004) pp. 1-4.

A SAUT Perspective Indication Unfair Gender Enrolment

Summary Statistics for Students at SAUT Main Campus Academic Year 2007/2008

ACADEMIC PROGRAMME	YEAR OF STUDY									Grand Total		
	YEAR 1			YEAR 2			YEAR 3					
	M	F	Total	M	F	Total	M	F	Total	M	F	Total
Faculty of Business Administration												
BBA	173	73	246	194	92	286	163	58	221	530	223	753
ADA	64	45	109	132	61	193	105	40	145	301	146	447
ADPLM	12	8	20	8	3	11	4	4	8	24	15	39
CA	77	58	135	0	0	0	0	0	0	77	58	135
CLSM	7	3	10	0	0	0	0	0	0	7	3	10
CHA	3	2	5	0	0	0	0	0	0	3	2	5
Sub Total	336	189	525	334	156	490	272	102	374	942	447	1389
Parallel Program												
BBA	0	0	0	16	9	25	14	7	21	30	16	46
ADA	19	8	27	25	8	33	13	11	23	57	27	84
ADPLM	0	0	0	2	1	3	2	1	3	4	2	6
Sub Total	19	8	27	43	18	61	29	19	47	91	45	136
Masters Program												
MAMC	12	10	22	4	2	6	6	2	8	22	14	36
MBA	34	6	40	0	0	0	0	0	0	34	6	40
Sub Total	46	16	62	4	2	6	6	2	8	56	20	76
Postgraduate Diploma												
PGDMC	0	0	0	0	0	0	0	0	0	0	0	0
PGDAF	15	6	21	0	0	0	0	0	0	15	6	21
Sub Total	15	6	21	0	0	0	0	0	0	15	6	21
Faculty of Social Sciences and Communications												
BAMC	54	71	125	117	128	245	156	114	270	327	313	640
BAEC	12	10	22	44	16	60	33	9	42	89	35	124
BASO	92	130	222	57	88	145	0	0	0	149	218	367
CJM	23	32	55	0	0	0	0	0	0	23	32	55
Sub Total	181	243	424	218	232	450	189	123	312	588	598	1186
Faculty of Education												
BAED	460	188	648	341	117	458	0	0	0	801	305	1106
Sub total	460	188	648	341	117	458	0	0	0	801	305	1106
Faculty of Laws												
LLB	101	42	143	0	0	0	0	0	0	101	42	143
Sub Total	101	42	143	0	0	0	0	0	0	101	42	143
Grand Total	1158	692	1850	940	525	1465	496	246	741	2594	1463	4057

SAUT 2007/2008 Enrolment as a Case Study

The numbers of girls/women enrolled is comparatively lower than that of boys/male. Is this accidental? Whom, should we blame or point fingers. The problem does not start here but at the BOP levels! Again, this problem goes deep down to the bad cultural and family attitudes in girls/females as a whole.

Gender Injustices in Macro Economic Planning and Budgeting
In recent years, the Tanzania Gender Network Program (TGNP) has been trying to identify certain areas in the Tanzanian government and society which hamper equal benefits and involvement of women particularly in Macro-Economic Planning and Budgeting.

Quite often, women are not given their right portion neither as beneficiaries of the national product nor as the stakeholders major drivers of development in the annual Tanzanian Budget. For example ministries line defense get higher financial support and expenditure rights than the ministries which deal with women in particular! Again, these are the symptoms. We need to see the deep-seated causes.

Gender Inequalities in Governance & Leadership Roles
In the last 15 years in Tanzania the number of women holding parliamentary seats has been increasing but that of males is exceeds more than ⅔. This mean, there is no proportionality.

Worse in the last new election of cabinet ministers in February, 2008 by President Jakaya Kikwete the number of women was substantially slashed down. However, the issue is far much deeper than we think. It goes down to BOP level. Are women given proper opportunities which fully and adequately equip with political competence and excellence right from the primary schools? Secondary schools? Definitely no.

These facts and figures, illustrate multiple socio-economic gender injustices and inequalities which discriminate and exploit women. Hence, making them economically poorer and poorer. These are symptoms.

Now let us try to identify the main deep-seated and hidden factors that is the causes for such a vicious and pathetic situation especially in Tanzania today. In other words, let us try to identify women worst enemies and later on look for best solutions and alternatives (Put Song: *The Power of A Woman* by Shaggy).

Womens' Worst Enemies: A Broader Picture

Among others the worst enemies which perpetuate such inequalities include the following below. Indeed, these enemies need to totally eradicated for a true change and transformation.

Bad Cultural Beliefs and Traditional African Practices

These constitute the top most enemies for women. Oppressive traditional beliefs in Tanzania's patriarchal ethnic groups are the major bottlenecks and hindrances for gender equity. They propagate illogical ideologies and dogmas which not only deprives women of their rights to own and manage resources and wealth, but also blinds them to consider themselves as a "weaker" sex and economically and managerially "tabula rasa"! They deny women their rights of education, ownership, governance etc. They deprive women of their rights and ability to control and enjoy the toil of their daily labour. E.g. among the Chagga women work for the entire process of coffee production till the carrying of coffee to the selling co-operative unions. However, men, simply walk along and behind to collect the money earned. The same applies in most of the patriarchal societies in Tanzania. Is there need to fight against this enemy from today? Absolutely yes.

Women Themselves

The second most dangerous enemies of women are fellow women. In her research, on the status of women in higher education management.[7]

---

[7] Nyokabi Kamau, "The Status of Women in Higher Education Management. A Study of One Private University in Kenya" in Eastern Africa Journal of Humanities and Sciences CUEA Vol. 2. No. 1 January-June 2002 p. 11

You women, (including myself) are the worst enemies of each other women seem to work against each other why do they keep complaining that they have no equal chances whereas, when they get to the top they do not support each other?

Such a suicidal feminist attitudes and cultures are permeate commonplace not only on the higher levels of societies but from the bottom upward!

NB: a) Refer to the denial of votes to fellow Presidential female Candidates in Kenya, Tanzania etc.
b) Refer to the "Exile Culture" at SAUT.

Men/Males/Husbands

Truly, research and ordinary life experience indicate that, men rank as the third worst enemies of women. This is seen in several discriminatory attitude and acts against women as a whole. Among others, continuous sexual abuse, household instrumentalisation of sex and love the use of women as mere instruments of production, sexual abuse and harassments, socio-ethnic rape, oppression, feminization of poverty, denial of womens rights for their dignity, and basic human rights education, leadership, "the myth of patriarchy," social exclusion, deprivation of women's economic and biological rights divorce revolution unjust remuneration provide concrete facts and figures as to how men rank as the third worst enemies to women. [Cfr- The Guardian Newspaper, Sunday, March 2, 2008 pp 1 & 2 for example – reported on the selling of the 13 years old girl Suzan Reuben by her uncle].

Cultural Globalization

This constitutes the fourth worst enemy against women. Today, many women especially in Africa and Tanzania in particular simply take copy and paste the Euro- American life styles without any reservation. They embrace them whole sale! E.g. Dressing code, "Mini skirts culture;" "the Thong culture," "the bikini culture," the "the thumb culture" expensive hair designs, lotions, perfumes, sun glasses, expensive cellular phones, cars, etc. All these corrupt and destroy the good African dressing culture as it appears only in the women's day for only 8,760 hours a year! How could women cry or adequate fight for their rights if they keep on being entangled in this new form of cultural slavery and blindness! Finally, are they not becoming the greatest losers instead of being the greatest winners?

Ignorance, Lack of Foresight, Solidarity, Courage and for Decision-making

These rank on the fifth position as far as women's greatest enemies, definitely, women's denial for in-depth and formative education make them passive indolent and in active socio- economically, politically and managerially. These exclude and paralyzed women totally.

Quite often women do not have the courage to reveal the daily domestic violence they experience. Truly, the reported case is far fewer than unreported ones.

In short, among others these enemies in particular disempower or disenable them to acquire the necessary intellectual as well as economical competence to own resources, wealth and plan for a dignified and high life, quality life as a whole. Hence, making their dreams never come true. Now let us see a way forward.

Which Way Forward? (The Business of Business Is Business): 10 Theses Suggestions and Alternatives

Truly, there are no easy solutions to deep and complex questions. Deep questions necessary need deep solutions. Moreover, it is an on-going socio-cultural, political and economic process which might take decades if not centuries.

Thesis One

There is urgent need especially for women in academia to address and focus mainly on the deeper causes or roots which deny women their socio-economic political and cultural rights especially from the personal, family and community levels first. The right to transformative education need to be priority one. Free education to women needs could be the best therapy. Cfr. The History of Austria by Queen Maria Theresa.

Thesis Two

Today, more than ever before, there is need for a "cultural deconstruction" to totally eliminate negative aspects in the patriarchal societies which promote gender inequalities as a whole. At this juncture the five worse enemies mentioned above should first be tackled. Indeed, among others, there is need collaboration and solidarity among all peoples, societies, and the government through critical, clear and creative thinking.

Thesis Three

In order to promote holistic socio-economic equity and sustainable development, in the present day highly competitive global economy, there is need for women in Tanzania in particular to try to open new avenue for other viable and economically lucrative activities. For instance, today, sports are increasingly becoming a highly profit making industry world wide. Refer Women Tennis World Players, Stars and Champions such as:

- e.g. - Maria Sharapora
  - Serena Williams
  - Anna Kournikora
  - Bia e Branca
  - Haley Cope

- Allison Stokke and others!
- The same applies in professional women football.

Let women here adopt the "Seed" approach of investment. That is Sports, Education, Economy and Decision Making = Mnemonically, "Seed."

Thesis Four

There is need to develop a new and truly caring economy in Tanzania which promotes and protects the values of equity and justice. In this economy, caring and care work are made visible, (re) valued, (re) affirmed, (re) produced and (re) distributed equitably.

Thesis Five

Laws particularly on equal ownership of land, wealth, capital need to be made and full implemented. Consequently, there is need to give equal access to premium land in projects micro-credit, technology access to knowledge market economic planning, savings, trade and industry. If the rules change eventually the attitude would change reforms in all sectors are necessary.

Thesis Six

There is need for women to learn from business success stories from fellow women from "Bottom of the Pyramid" (BOP) and Self-Help Group (SHG) locally and globally.

N.B: India offers the best and concrete examples. Refer the women run economic project such as:

a) Energy for everyone
b) The Annapurna Salt Project
c) Homes for the Poor – The CEMEX Story
d) The Jaipur Foot Story

All these and others offer concrete case stories of women successful innovations and entrepreneurship at BOP! Women in academia particular have a duty to facilitate this dream!

Thesis Seven

There is urgent need for women scholars to a new culture of positive thinking critically and courageously especially about their competence, in social transformation and in bringing a difference politically, economically, socially, technologically, culturally, environmentally, ethically and religiously.

Thesis Eight

There is need to adopt as an excellent women Manifesto, Mary's Song of Liberation echoed in her Magnificat Luke 1:46-55. Indeed, women regardless of their religious faiths or traditions, could greatly and deeply get inspired through and by this most powerful biblical song sung by Mary Mother of Jesus of Nazareth.

> My soul glorifies the Lord" and my sprit rejoices in God my Savior, for he has been mindful of the humble state of his servant. From now on all generations will call me blessed, for the Might One has done great thing/for me. His mercy extends to those who fear him, from generation to generation. He has performed mighty deeds with his arm; he has scattered those who are proud in their inmost thoughts. He has brought down rulers from their thrones but has lifted up the humble. He has filled the hungry with good things/but has sent the rich away empty. He has helped his servant Israel, remembering to be merciful to Abraham and his descendants forever, even as he said to our fathers."Amen/ Halleluya.

Thesis Nine

True women's solidarity in Tanzania and Africa as a whole could be one of the best and effective means or tools in bringing about gender equity, justice and true empowerment among women. This could offer on chances for going formation and education, and awareness building through talks, workshops, seminars etc.

Thesis Ten

There is urgent need especially by the government and non-governmental organizations in Tanzania to institute and enforce equity policies which promote and protect basic human rights and especially those of marginalized women covering all aspects socio-economic, cultural and academic life.

Let me conclude by saying that we still have a long way to go. Nonetheless, right thinking, right judging and right the courage to act feeling among scholars, women and men paralleled with be the stepping stone for a new day, a new epoch of justice, equity and solidarity. The "Business of Business is Business." Let us start now.

References

African Development Bank, Tanzania-Multi Sector Country Gender Profile 2005, p.9.

Aruna Gnanadason, Kanyoro Musimbi (eds), Women Violence and Non-Violent Change, 1996. Geneva, WCC Publications.

Athena, K. Peratta, A Caring Economy Geneva, WCC Publications, 2005.

Nyokabi Kamau, "The Status of Women in Higher Education Management. A Study of One Private University in Kenya" in Eastern Africa Journal of Humanities and Sciences CUEA Vol. 2. No. 1 January-June, 2002.

World Development Indicators, 2004.

Chapter Five

THE ANATOMY OF WITCHCRAFT AND ITS IMPACT ON HUMAN LIFE IN TANZANIA TODAY

Preliminary Remarks

Today, more than ever before, human life in all its aspects is increasingly being threatened by both natural and man made threats. Among others, in Tanzania, there has been in last few years in particular, ever increasing and alarming cases, and events indicating a destructive witchcraft hysteria and crisis countrywide. This has been more prevalent in some regions especially in Mwanza, Geita district, Mbeya and Sumbawanga. From an economic point of view, today we live in a world which commercializes everything. As such profit regardless of life, values, ethics is the rule of the day, rule of the jungle.

Worse still, today, it is increasingly becoming almost quite common to witness many Tanzanian elites, and scholars of different professions, caliber and status succumbing into this destructive syndrome and culture. These include some politicians, entrepreneurs, media experts, business managers, economists, sociologists, medical doctors, lecturers etc. This paper tries to make a brief indepth post-mortem and analysis particularly on the deeper causes of the ever growing witchcraft bomb or disaster among many Tanzanians today.

Aim

This chapter tries to search and identify the hidden causative facts, realities and factors. Further, as perspective chapter, it calls for deeper solutions against the so-called Life-Destroying Witchcraft-Syndrome (LDWS) today. In short, witchcraft has now become a lucrative profit making enterprise (industry) among many people especially to many Tanzanians today.

Terminology

From time immemorial, witchcraft, ("Uchawi") has been called different names and terminologies by different societies both local and global. E.g. "Usawi" – (Chagga) "Ushirikina" – (Swahili) – "Mfiti" – (Chewa), "Ulogi" – (Nyamwezi), "Uhani" – (Pogoro), "Obulosi" – (Gita), "Uthawi" – (Pare). "Juju" (Igbo Nigeria), "Nndosi" – (Nyakyusa), "Uwoyi" – (Kamba), "Bulosi" – (Luhya), "Omlugi" – (Haya), devil worship, black magic, astrology scientology, horuskopus, etc. For the sake of proper understanding and clarity, Laurenti Magesa considers witchcraft as "the greatest wrong or destructiveness on earth of which all other wrongs are but variations emanations or manifestations"[1] Professor Magesa goes a step further to unveil the effects of witchcraft by saying:

> Most of the time suffering, sickness and death have their origin in witchcraft. If religious leaders have any influence on the people, then it consists in counteracting acts, or even intentions, of witchcraft for witchcraft constitutes the perversion of everything that is good and desired in human beings; it is the personification or incarnation of all that is anti-life and therefore the ultimate enemy of life on earth.[2]

On the global perspective especially today, John S. Pobee a prominent west African anthropologist and scholar quotes Bridget Finney in the Time Magazine who claims that witchcraft and witchcraft beliefs and cults are "on the rise, New Ageism, Satanism and everything to do with occultism…Rather than turn to God, we try to fill the hole in our souls with money, prestige, sex, alcohol, food, pop culture, almost everything. Where does this lead us? To a decaying society."[3]

---

[1] Laurenti Magesa, African Religion The Moral Traditions of Abundant Life (Nairobi: Pauline Publications, Africa), 2002 p.69.
[2] Ibid p.69.
[3] Time Magazine, 5th May 1997:6.

Justification

The specific reasons for this paper is necessarily to promote a preventive pro-life culture against the ever increasing culture of evil and suffering resulting from witchcraft and witchcraft beliefs, practices or tendencies. Indeed, by the anatomy (Greek "anatomos") we mean, the very causative inner nature of witchcraft. In short, as rational beings we need to draw the line between what is right from what is wrong, what is life-protecting from life destroying, what brings hope from what brings despair. In short, this chapter tries to rediscover the vital forces of life, abundant life, against all traditions of malice, envy, jealousy, mischief, vengeance, malevolent, treachery, insecurity, evil, idolatry, worship of devil, mammon, sorcery, superstition and death. In short, it tries to promote a pro-active pro-life stance especially among university scholars and professionals.

This chapter is divided into three major parts. In the first part, an attempt will be made to unveil the hidden causative factors, behind the witchcraft crisis today and particularly in Tanzania. The second part tries to give a way forward. That is, all-round integral alternatives and solutions to this crisis which seems to get out of control soon!

The Anatomy of Witchcraft: Some Deeper Causes

At this juncture, let us ask ourselves the following questions.

- What deeper hidden factors or causes are behind the witchcraft hysteria or syndrome, or in Tanzania today?
- What do witches aim at?
- What psychological, economic religious and spiritual factors are contributing to this highly destructive wave of witchcraft? Let us now try to identify these elements.
- Do they really want to help or make their clients rich? Better? Happier? Mores successful than themselves?

Among others, the following life-destroying forces form the basic pillars and characteristic elements behind the ever growing threat of witchcraft syndrome particularly in Tanzania today. These are encapsulated and echoed in the following ten hypotheses as developed by Dr. Aidan G. Msafiri (2008).

First Hypothesis: Globalization and Spread of Evil among Peoples and Societies Today

Today, more than ever before, many people are trying to avoid Kant's theory of categorical imperative: "Always do good and Avoid Evil". Many are simply becoming schizophrenic sadists. They willingly struggle to spread and inflict suffering, pain and eventually death (biologically, economically, socially, psychologically etc) through natural and supernatural means. Scholars call this "the human incarnation of evil".[4] The day-to-day sad scenarios locally and globally attest to this hypothesis.

Second Hypothesis: Creation of Insecurity and Excessive Psychological Fears (Worries) Among Humans

This is a very strong current strategy employed by witches in order to get more psychologically paralyzed, disturbed and disoriented people who would in turn seek solutions from them (witches). Hence, increasing the number of their clients every hour, every day, every week, every month etc. Witches are very good in creating the so-called "mikwala". That is, very shocking situations or scenarios! Experts in the fields of psychology and psychoanalysis say that almost 90% of the things which disturb people never happen in one's life time!

Scientific evidence shows that about 75% of the human diseases have their connection or origin from psychological disturbances particularly fears, worriers, hatred, bitterness, enmity, etc. Wighard

---

[4] Magesa Laurenti (2002) p.179.

Strehlow (1998) asserts that the disturbed "psyche" (soul) makes the human body very fragile and full of enmity like that of a frence dog, tries to retaliate and bite someone or something.[5]

From a current Tanzanian "Sitz in Leben", many people, the poor, the rich, the illiterate, the educated, Christians as well as non-Christians are living in an ocean of multiple fears. As one psychologist says: "there is no vacuum in nature", so these people try to search for all means to do away from such fears or insecurities – politically, socially, economically, sexually, medically, professionally, intellectually etc.

Briefly, witches try to suggest or prescribe very extraordinary gestures symbols, languages and contradictory alternatives using rare objects in order to fully "convince" their clients!

e.g. Prescription of: Crocodile's Sweat!!
- Snakes lungs!
- Albinos skins, organs, hair, etc.
- Human sexual/private organs and the list goes on and on and on.

Nyamiti Charles (1995) admits that, evil can be effected by symbolic gestures such as curse, spell, or imitative magic for him evil is both anti-life and anti-communitarian.

Third Hypothesis: Contract with Devil (Satan) – ("Mkataba na Shetani")

It is a real fact that, devil (satan) exists. God exists too! As an anti-life spiritual being, the devil can make a contract with humans. Such a contract has to be fulfilled by very life-destroying requirements from the devil to his/her client. The devil can promise and deliver riches, money and prosperity to someone who would daily perform highly

---

[5] Wigrand Strehlow, Heilen Mit der Kraft der Seele, (Freiburg im Breisgau: Baner, 1998) page 342.

evil deeds e.g. every year offering of one's sons, daughters, wife, relatives, other humans' blood etc. These are the deadly "terms" and "conditions" of devil contract and devil worship. Today, this is a sad endemic highly widespread among particularly rich city dwellers and business class in Tanzania and Africa today. Nonetheless, findings show that such riches or seeming prosperity do not last long at all. Usually, they disappear after a while!

Thesis Four: Ignorance and Lack of Foresight Among Many Tanzanians

Indeed, ever growing ignorance and lack of a foresight and critical mind among many citizens (both illiterate and literate) are immensely contributing to the spread of the anti-life witchcraft culture in the Tanzanian societies. As one prominent scholar once said "If you think knowledge/education is expensive, try ignorance." Truly, ignorance is very expensive particularly when one makes a critical post-mortem of its consequences! Moreover, as the famous Swahili adage or axiom goes: "wajinga ndiyo waliowao" (Literally translated as, fools will be the loosers!)

Thesis Five: A Deadly Killing (Murder) Syndrome of Innocent People

From a Tanzanian perspective and particularly in Mwanza Region, recent research findings indicate an exponential increase of people killed in connection to witchcraft beliefs and practices. These included particularly women, and fewer men.

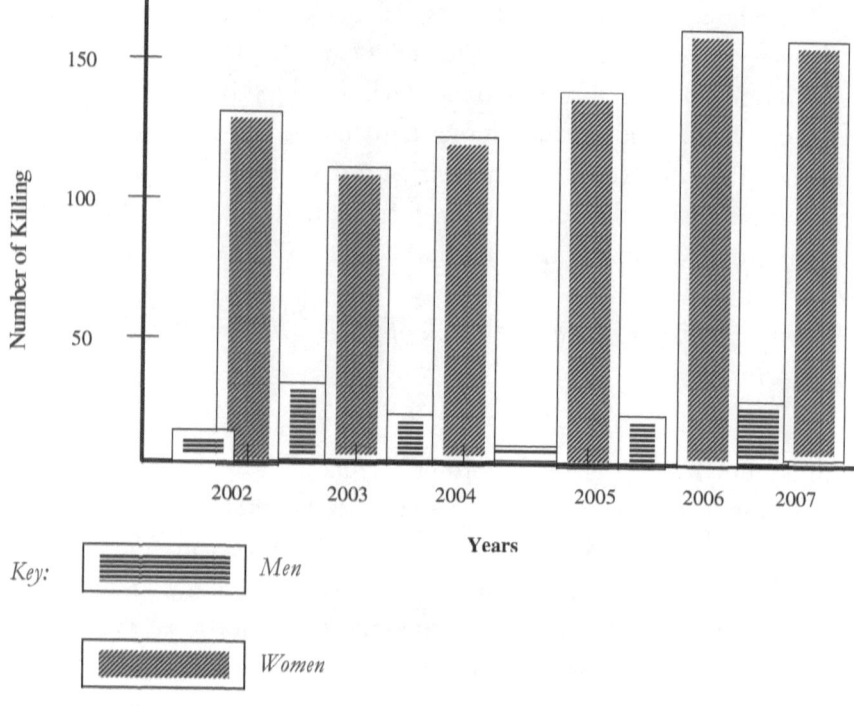

Source: *The 2008 Symposium On "Juhudi za Pamoja Dhidi ya Mauaji Katika Mkoa Wetu wa Mwanza, page 9.*

The above drawn graphs, shows the facts and figures of the approximate human killing of the innocent ranging from the year 2002 to 2007.

In this year (2008), this killings' syndrome has assumed other tragic dimensions and proportions especially by killing albinos. Let me identify some few concrete cases.

First on the 17th April 2006 at around 19:30 pm at Nyahunge village, one albino called Ariph Amon, 35 years old was brutally killed by bandits organs of his body were taken to witches.[6]

---

[6] Kongamano Kuhusu "Mauaji yatokanayo na Imani za Kishirikina, RPC, Mwanza 17 – 18 March, 2008 p.2.

Second, on the 23rd May 2007 at around 1:30 am at Mwamboku village, Misungwi district, an albino called Shitakelelwa Chitoberwa was killed by an unknown people and took organs of his body away soon.[7]

Third, on the 15th August 2007 at around 21:00 p.m., at Buharahara village, Geita district, a gang of 5 people invaded the home of James Charles (37) and took his two sons who are albinos Remy (12) and Zakaria (7) and disappeared with them. Todate, these children have never been found![8]

Fourth, on the 3rd October 2007 at midnight, around Shigunga village, in Geita district, Rwegamoyo Kilanga (62) an albino, was brutally murdered and his two arms were taken away.[9]

Fifth, on the 11th March, 2008 at around 20:00 p.m. at Nyamarulu village, an albino girl called Zawadi Magindu (22) was brutally killed and her two legs were chopped off and taken away.[10]

In short, these and several other very pathetic incidences on the killings of albinos especially in Mwanza region, allude to be caused by the witchcraft syndrome.

Sixth Hypothesis: *Ever Growing Economic Hardships, Inflation and Abject Poverty*

Today, more than 85% of all Tanzanians are earning less than 1 US $ per day. That means, less than Tsh. 1,200/=. The prices of foodstuffs and other basic needs are simply sky rocketing. The poor who constitute the majority of the population are the worst hit. These include the poor witches living very miserable life especially in the poorest areas and regions of Tanzania.

---

[7] Kongomano Kuhusu, (Ibid) p.3.
[8] Ibid p.3
[9] Ibid p.3
[10] Ibid p.3

Due to this, most of the poor people are searching for short-cuts and easy ways to get money or wealth. On the other hand, the poor witches are commercializing and "advertising" their quite longed for "service" and "expertise" as an immediate and short-cut solution. Consequently, creating a dependency syndrome on them (witches).

Further, findings show that, many people especially in Mwanza city and region as a whole, are totally convinced that any economic or financial success has either to come from witchcraft or at least has to be related to witchcraft beliefs or practices. This is really pathetic. The following Swahili quotation resonates the deadly belief:

Mafanikio katika maisha kwa watu wengi wa Mwanza hudhani kuwa ni lazima yatokane au yahusishwe na imani za kishirikina na sio utendaji kazi kupitia njia sahihi za halali na za kisheria katika kujipatia maishamazuri. Imani hizo za kishirikina huusishwa na kujikita zaidi katika nyanja za biashara, uvuvi, upatikanaji wa madini, elimu, michezo na hata kujipatia nafasi mbalimbali za uongozi. Kwa mfano hivi sasa Mauaji mapya ya albino yanayoendelea kutokea yanapata kasi kutoka kwa waganga wasio waaminifu wanaowarubuni wateja wao kwamba ili ufanikiwe ni lazima viungo vya albino vipatikane. Na upatikanaji wa viungo hivyo ni lazima mauaji yatekelezwe[11]

Thesis Seven: The Massive and Wanton Spread of Witchcraft Movies/Films from Nigeria

In the last ten years in particular, witchcraft moves and films particularly from Nigeria have been a growing centre of attraction and attention hypnotizing both youth, elites and common people in Tanzania in particular. Among other very thrilling Nigeria movies, films, CD, VCDs, DVDs which have been promoting the witchcraft culture and syndrome among many people in Tanzania are the following:

"The Price of Sacrifice"
"The Billionaires Club"

---

[11] Ibid, "Kongamano" – p.13

"The Free Side Mission"
"My Love"
"The End of the Wicked"
"The Power of Love"
"Married to a Witch"
"Remember your Mother"
"Hour of Grace"
"Conspiracy"
"Hatred"
"A Cry for Help" etc.

All these and other movies have immensely contributed to the present day Tanzanian witchcraft crisis and syndrome in particular.

Hypothesis Eight: Secret, Systematic - Slow Killing Tricks

Quite often, witches use very secrete and clandestine maneouvres which could cause gradual death to someone especially by secrete poisoning procedures through food, water, drink, air, etc. This can be done by using different natural or man-made elements, substances, herbs or minerals, found on nature. Eventually, they claim to be "mysterious" cause of such very secret deaths. Therefore, manipulating the truth.

Hypothesis Nine: Absence of Distinction between Good/Legal Medicine Expertise and Traditional Healing

Today, witches are trying to amalgamate and sycronise their "industry" with good traditional healing procedures. At this juncture, for example in Mwanza region, there are about 700 legally registered traditional healers/ medicine men. These have license from the government. However, most of these, if not all do not make a distinction between the two! Some traditional healers misuse this, and quite often manipulate girls or women to have sex with them.

As one informant said, such tricky traditional healers tell the female client "Nitakuosha mwenyewe" "(I will wash you myself") The woman would literary remain naked to be washed with traditional medicine. The process of washing also includes massaging of different parts of the body including sexual organs. Once the client is well stimulated, then the healer "completes" the treatment by having sex with her ("Kusindikiza dawa").[12]

It has also been affirmed that, some of the traditional herbs or substances are stimulants to arouse women for sex. Clients may be urged to stay at the "healers" homestead for several months while taking such clandestine products!

Hypothesis Ten: The Godlessness and Secularist Culture Today

Admittedly, the lives of many people in today's world Christians and non-Christians are shifting away from the author of life (creator), the epicenter, care taker and provider of life, that is God, the Intelligent Designer (I.D). They embrace a very powerful secularist materialistic culture of idolatry. To many, life is simply void. It is meaningless. Consequently, they endlessly search for "something" or "someone" outside the True God and Creator to fill that gap, that "lacuna", that void!!! In modern Tanzanian parlance and "Sitz im Lebern", witches are spreading a powerful culture of idolatry and false prophetism. That is, the spread of "TV za Asili". Why can't they show us what is happening in Europe, US, Afghanistan? Iraq, Russia, Zimbambwe, etc? Refer the false religious sects or movements in Tanzania Today – E.g. 2008 in Mbeya Region! In short, as a modern and powerful type of idolatry, witchcraft beliefs and practices are destroying not only biological life, but spiritual life which gives deeper sense, meaning, orientation and anchorage to all humans regardless of their age, sex, religion etc.

Having critically analysed and unveiled these ten hypotheses of the anatomy of witchcraft industry in Tanzania today, let us forge for concluding remarks and possible alternatives.

---

[12] Ibid, "Kongamano" "under Socio-Cultural Practices". p.4

Some Concluding Remarks, Reflections and Recommendations

Truly, the present day ever growing witchcraft crisis, hysteria and syndrome need urgent but deeper solutions. Indeed, this crisis occasions a real challenge to all Tanzanians and humans from all walks of life. Among others, the following solutions or alternatives need special and immediate attention and priority in particular.

We need collaborative solidarity, courage, and culture to say: "No to Death and Yes to Life" particularly returning back to God Cfr: Demt: 18:10-13 "Let no one be found among you who sacrifices his son or daughter in the fine, who practices divination or sorcery, interprets omens, engage in witchcraft, or casts spells or who is a medium or spiritists or who consults the dead. Anyone who does these things is detestable to the LORD, and because of these detestable practices the LORD your God will drive out those nations before you. You must be blameless before the LORD your God" (Refer also Gal. 5:19-23 Col. 3:5, 1 Cor 6:18, Eph. 5:3 1 Th. 43) In short, we can never ever get rid of this spiritual crisis without putting God, faith and ethics on the first place!!! People who have not been affected by this deadly syndrome need special catechesis and encouragement.

We need today, more than ever before, to rethink anew, personally and collectively especially on the importance of the three theological virtues of Faith, Hope and Charity (Love).

We need to rediscovery particularly the basic ethical and religious values and virtues especially fear of God, prudence, true worship, prayer truthfulness, etc.

We need to reinforce civil as well as human laws and by-laws which protect and promote universal human and dignity and rights. Hence, fostering proactive and preventive approaches, attitudes and cultures against the emerging anti-life culture as a whole.

We need to endlessly and constantly fight against poverty and abject misery among many Tanzanians and Africans as a whole. Hence, collectively we need to promote true and integral (holistic) human development. This should necessarily start on the individual level particularly by fighting against the current Tanzanian cultures of laziness, irresponsibility, fraud, corruption, ("ufisadi") and inaccountability, injustices, oppression, marginalization etc.

As rational human beings, we need to rethink particularly as regards the rational use of the human intellect especially in thinking clearly, critically and creatively. In short the need true intellectual maturity and self-affirmation.

We need to agree with the fact as Fr. Titus Amigu affirms: "Uchawi hautishi, ni usanii". (witchcraft is simply a comedy!) Therefore, the need to develop a true sense and culture of confidence, trust and all-round competence against the virtual threats and unfounded fears alluded to witchcraft.

As Africans, we need to rethink on promoting the values of solidarity (community), totality, vitality and sustainability and abundant life (John 10:10). As Professor Charles Nyamiti (1995) aptly remarks: "Fullness of life is obtained through vital communion with openness (relationality) to the world of spirits (God – the Supreme Being, ancestors....), fellow human beings and the world of nature.

In short, we are all argued to do good and avoid evil as Immanuel Kant's Theory of Categorical Imperative suggests. Lastly, today *a systematic globalization of what is good* is of paramount importance against the ever spreading destructive "Screen Culture" (TV Culture) which propagates evil, suffering, hopelessness and death. Let each person, each family, each school, each community, society, each university and all people of all religions and of good will begin this work now!

References

Jamhuri ya Muungano wa Tanzania Ofisi ya Waziri Mkuu (TAMISEMI), 2008: Kongamano Kuhusu Juhudi za Pamoja Dhidi ya Mauaji katika Mkoa Wetu wa Mwanza, 17 na 18 Machi.

Magesa Laurent, 2002: *African Religion: The Moral, Traditions of Abundant Life*, Nairobi; Pauline Publications Africa.

Magesa Laurent, 2006: "Witchcraft: A Pastoral Guide in African Ecclesial Review" *AFER* Vol. 48, Number 3, September.

Munga Tehenan, 2007: *Uchawi: Unavyokupata na Kujikinga*, Faji.

Nyamiti Charles, 1995: *The Problem of Evil in African Traditional Culture and Today's African Inculturation and Liberation.* In African Christian Studies CUEA-Publication Nairobi.

Pobee John S., 1998: *Celebrating the Jubilee of the World Council of Churches*, Accra, Assempa Publishers.

Strehlow Wigrad, 1998: "Heilen Mit Der Kraft der Seele" *Freiburg im Breisgau Baner.*

www.ingramcontent.com/pod-product-compliance
Lightning Source LLC
Chambersburg PA
CBHW021132300426
44113CB00006B/392